Cover Him

Cover Him

*Caring for the Hidden Needs,
Thoughts, and Feelings of The Man You Love*

Roderick Hairston | Strong Family Press

Cover Him: Caring for the Hidden Needs, Thoughts, and Feelings of the Man You Love
By Rod Hairston

ISBN: 9781720480419 Paperback Print
ISBN: 13: 978-1-7339006-0-7 Hardcover

Printed in the United States of America

This book is dedicated to Master Chief Robert "Pop" Boyd, my stepfather of twenty-seven years. Your courage to keep climbing the stairs even while your heart was failing has given me the courage to keep writing, teaching, preaching, and loving. On October 21, 2018 you climbed the top step and you're now with Jesus. "The steps of a good man are ordered by the Lord" (Psalm 37:23). I salute you.

Foreword

Pastor Rod Hairston has a long history of studying the relationships between men and women through a biblical lens. His experience as a husband, father, pastor, NFL chaplain, counselor, and community leader enhances his insight and down-to-earth wisdom. *Cover Him* is written out of a desire to see healthy, respectful, joyful, helpful relationships flourish. After writing about the ways men should support and encourage women in *Cover Her*, Pastor Hairston turns the tables to write in practical, honest, gritty ways about the ways women can support and encourage men without losing their own dignity as children of God.

If you are looking for common sense, real world, no beating-around-the-bush counsel, this book is for you. It is a clarion call for women to use their unique and God-given voices to speak truth and love to the men in their lives. It will provoke healthy conversations, describe healthy boundaries, and promote healthy male-female relationships.

I strongly recommend it.

Jay Barnes
President, Bethel University

Endorsements

Cover Him is practical and insightful. A clear and concise guide to understanding the needs of my husband, it has answered questions that I have had since getting married about how to love a man and bring out the best in him. I am thankful for a coaching guide that is honest and gives real and very familiar scenarios.

Dionne Boldin | 14-Year NFL Wife

Cover Him is spot on. It says all the things a man will very rarely say to a woman. It provides a deeper understanding into the heart of a man.

Anquan Boldin | 14-Year NFL Veteran, Q81 Foundation President

Rod Hairston has written a timely and important book that will help close the relationship gaps between men and women in general and married couples in particular. Ladies, if you want to know how to bring out the best in the man you love, we joyfully commend *Cover Him* to you.

Benjamin and Kirsten Watson | 15-Year NFL Veteran

"*Cover Him*, is loaded with practical tools and words of wisdom that any woman can use to support the man or men in her life. Whether married or mothering sons, the principles in this book, when applied, will help chart the course to success for the men you love."

Trina Jenkins | Director of Family Ministries
First Baptist Church of Glenarden

Acknowledgements

My life has been surrounded by brilliant, strong, godly, resilient women who bear great responsibility for anything I've accomplished that is of note. I've been covered in every way on some level by each of them.

Sheri Hairston, my unwavering partner, soul mate, and bride of twenty-eight years. I can't imagine where I'd be without your friendship, affirmation, constant support, and warmth. Thank you for suffering long with me as I started, stopped, and restarted the manuscript for this book. You have been the epitome of what *Cover Him* is all about. I pray countless women will learn from your powerful example and that men around the world will become who they were made to be because of it. Thank you for covering me with prayer, companionship, understanding, and so much more. I honor and adore you.

Betty Hairston-Boyd—better known as Mom—your dedication to your boys is the reason I walk in my gifts. Thank you for nurturing my interests, passions, and curiosities as a little boy. Thank you for being there without fail to give your supporting presence. You've championed me— the son, the young man, the husband, the father, the preacher, the writer. I thank God for you, and I thank Him for using you to bring me into this amazing world. Your strength is indomitable. May God make your latter years even greater than your former years.

Aunt Jean, you covered me, literally, with Stride-Rite shoes, Easter outfits, a car for high school dates, prayers, and a model of discipleship. Your support of Mom and your commitment to her boys cannot be underestimated. My curiosity about God and the way of salvation was sparked by your sudden and clear dedication to the way of Jesus. Thank you for staying steadfast on the journey, for sowing seed after seed into my life and ministry, and for celebrating my commitment to being a man of God, a dedicated husband, and a fully engaged father. I cherish your words, your spirit, and your place in my life.

Leah, Maya, Tyla, and Jeremy. Three exceptional ladies and one extraordinary gentleman. I don't have the words to tell you what you mean to me. My greatest joy and honor, next to marrying your mother, has been to be your father. You make me proud. And you make me want to make you proud. I feel covered by your never-ending grace toward me when I've missed the mark in your lives. I'm grateful that your journey into adulthood has come with an open invitation: you've welcomed me along to share what I can. You've said, "Dad, your voice matters to us." Thank you for being extraordinary human beings whose love for Jesus is indisputable. May He continue to cover you, and may He use you to cover those He's entrusting to your lives and leadership.

Finally, thank you, Team Messiah of Messiah Community Church. Thank you for releasing me to exercise my passion to write. I couldn't do what God has called me to do—to help marriages and generations of families—without your tireless, sacrificial support. There is absolutely no way. You hold up my hands with your prayers and lighten my load with your focused and dedicated service to Jesus. It is an absolute joy to serve as your Pastor, friend, mentor, and visionary leader. I'm humbled that God lets me lead people who are far more capable than I am in so many ways. May God give you the desires of your hearts and pour His undying favor upon you and your dreams.

With love and deep affection,
Roderick L. Hairston

Introduction

In the era of the #MeToo movement, the number of men who are coming out of the shadows is growing. Men today are told to man-up and act like men with few models and roadmaps to guide them. Our colossal failures cannot be overlooked, and neither can excuses be offered. Because of this, in a time when we're often put down, men desperately need to be uplifted, encouraged, and guided.

Women play a vital role in the progress and success of men, but they are often at a loss to know how to support, help, and inspire them. That's where this book comes in. *Cover Him* is a roadmap for every lady longing for direction to know how to help the men in her life to be their best and who really wants to know how to relate to them in a more effective and healthy way. Consider it a coaching manual. The insights it contains are keys or principles. Keep in mind, however, that not every key can or should be used all the time, in every situation. These are not laws. Rather view the insights as coaching points from a male friend whose experiences you can trust, biblical principles shared by a pastor, or brotherly advice from someone who cares that his sister be equipped for a lifelong relationship to the man she has or will someday marry.

While the angle of the book's discussion is tilted largely toward married women, its principles are not exclusive to the marriage relationship. Mothers can translate many of the principles and keys to their relationships with their developing or adult sons. Sisters can see the principles through the lens of their relationships with their brothers or close male friends.

My sincere prayer is that *Cover Him* will bless relationships between women and men in unprecedented and unexpected ways. I pray that women will be richly blessed and rewarded as they use the keys this book offers. And I pray men will be blessed to experience the life-giving force of women who have taken their rightful place as strong builders and influencers for good, for God.

Before we begin, let me be perfectly clear. With every principle we share in this book, we presuppose functional, respectful relationships. A woman cannot and should not cover someone who is abusive and disrespectful. Love him, care for him, and want what's best for him, but do not aid or enable any man's destructive and damaging behaviors.

Where I discuss sex anywhere in this book, it is always with the clear understanding that "Marriage is honorable among all, and the bed undefiled; but fornicators and adulterers God will judge" (Hebrews 13:4 NKJV). If you're unmarried, wait for God's timing. You cannot apply God's principles to relationships outside His acceptable boundaries and expect His blessing.

This book has been in the conceptual stage for too many years to mention. After *Cover Her*, many women asked me to write *Cover Him*. I tried. I even attempted to preach a series of messages by the same title. But I couldn't gain clarity about what women wanted to know. I was also concerned that such a title and such a book might come across as a chauvinistic attempt to put women in their place. Something I certainly never would intend. (I love my wife, daughters, and mom too much.) I found it very difficult to find the language and the most hearable tones for this book because I'm sensitive to the cultural tensions and the fallout from so many hurts men have caused. The stories of sexual abuse in entertainment, the Catholic church, the Evangelical movement, corporate America, and beyond continue to emerge, seemingly *ad infinitum*. I wonder when it will end. But alas! I recognize that not all men are guilty of these painful, damaging failures. There are many men who cherish and protect the women and children around them, but who long to be understood by those very women.

This book is written with those realities in mind, but I'm certain that I cannot write it without offending someone. The subject matter is sensitive, and finding a tone that fits every reader—well, that's impossible. But if you dare to venture through the pages of *Cover Him*, my hope and prayer is that you'll sense my deep respect for women, men, and the relationship that we were made to enjoy together—something mutual, joyful, and deeply satisfying. So I decided to take the risk in the hopes that *Cover Him* would be like a coaching manual, not a dogma, and certainly not a disrespect to women in any way. I fully acknowledge that women have been treated with inferiority for way too long—oppressed, abused, objectified, and minimized far too often.

What sparked me to pick up the initial outline and begin writing again after several years was a nudge from God that said, "It's time." Then I began to hear from women again after our first Cover Her Conference. Their consistent message was, "Pastor, we need help. Our men don't talk to us. We don't know what they need or how to support them." So I began to think of all the conversations and counseling sessions I've had with men. I reached out to a small group of men I'm mentoring and asked, "What would you like the ladies in your life to understand about you? How would you like them to support you as a man?"

What they wrote back in a matter of hours was powerful, clear, heartfelt, and in some cases, heartbreaking. Men long to be understood and supported. They long to be encouraged to be their best. But truthfully, many men feel beat down, discouraged, unsupported, and misunderstood.

Please know that none of the keys shared in this book is an indictment of anyone. Ladies, you are not ultimately responsible for any failed decision the man in your life has made or may make. But my hope is that knowing how to support him on the way to an important decision, through a tough season, or after a dismal failure will yield abundant and pleasurable fruit in his life and in your relationship.

So let's get to it, already. How do you bring out the best in the men you value and love? What will it take to care for those hidden, often unspoken, thoughts, needs, and feelings that he lives with day after day?

I hope that in some way, this book will empower women who want to understand us men and our needs better, to stand equipped and encouraged, perhaps to talk us out of our own malaise. I hope this book will help women to effectively point out to the men in their lives the untapped potential many of us have allowed to lie dormant. Ladies, we need you—all of you—your strengths, your voices, your brilliant insights, your support, and your perspectives.

Table of Contents

1

Affirm Him:
Let Him Know He Has What It Takes

Positive words, a wink, a thumb-up, and applause go a long way for everyone. We all feel better having received genuine, unsolicited affirmation. It has a way of brightening our countenance and lifting our heads. Affirming words and gestures encourage, inspire, and motivate people of all ages, sexes, and walks of life. And men, to the surprise of some ladies, are no exception. Like everyone else, a man needs voices of affirmation and inspiration in his life—someone who believes in him, who knows him, who respects him, and who is unreservedly for him. If you're the lady in his life, I can assure you that he wants and needs your cheering spirit and your cheering voice to affirm him.

Track with me for a moment, ladies. It's so unfortunate that the supporting role of cheerleaders in American culture has been cheapened. It's not surprising and quite understandable that most women frown upon the notion of being a man's cheerleader. Professional sports cheerleading has become synonymous with exploitation, manipulation, and scandal. I know, having served fourteen years as an NFL chaplain. Watching spectators in the stands and players on the sideline whenever the cheerleaders took to the field was always heart-wrenching for me. I usually turned my back to the show to separate myself and my thoughts from the gawking and ogling that commenced like second nature the moment the pompoms were lifted to the music. Cheerleading has devolved to epitomize abuse and objectification. No woman wants or needs either of those. No woman should ever be viewed so disrespectfully and dishonorably. And no man should tolerate it. I thank God for the #MeToo movement for bringing much-needed attention to entrenched sexism in our nation!

But let's be careful not to throw out the proverbial baby with the bath water. While the sexualized role of professional sports cheerleaders has fed the male-dominated environs of sports and promoted chauvinism, we should be clear: *cheering* is not cheerleading. One thing is not the other. One communicates value. The other devalues—both the cheerleader and the onlooker. One fosters God-honoring relationship. The other dehumanizes and incites fantasies that undo meaningful relationships. Cheerleading is not cheering. Men can (and should) do without cheerleaders. But a man needs a person who believes in his potential and is willing to cheer him on to fulfill it.

Whether we men say it or not, we long to be affirmed. We need it. We thrive on it. Many of us are deprived of its very oxygen in our lives. We're panting with thirst for it and deprived of the nourishment it feeds our souls. And what's the impact of low or no affirmation? For many men I've counseled, their confidence is languishing—waning by the hour. Feeling lost, frustrated, and desperate, anger is slowly building a channel in some of our psyches. One word of affirmation could be the difference between a breakdown or a breakthrough.

Men are calling out for affirmation, but many can't seem to get the women who matter most to them to understand. "Be my cheerleader. Encouragement goes a long way," wrote one of my mentees when asked what he needs most from his wife. Another wrote, "Encourage me to step out of my comfort zone as it relates to my faith. Challenge me to grow, to serve, and to take chances for the Kingdom." In short, these men want to know, "Do you believe in me? If you do, then tell me."

Affirmation is not ego stroking (okay, maybe it is, in a sense) but inside every man is a button, which when pressed propels him, lifts him, and motivates him. That button is what I call his *A-Button*—his affirmation button. It reminds him that he *can,* even if he hasn't yet. It reminds him that it's worth trying again, even when he has failed previously. It draws out his potential, bolsters his confidence, and reminds him that he has something meaningful to offer the world.

The Necessity of Affirmation
His dad was not in the picture. As far as anyone knows, his dad had no interest in the spiritual journey that his son was embarking on. Like so many boys in our day and time, he grew up surrounded by women. That's

not an indictment. It was not a strike against him. It was just the facts. And thank God for those ladies! His mother and grandmother taught him to love and follow Jesus at an early age.

As a young man in his late teens or early twenties, his hunger for ministry became more apparent. And when the traveling evangelist came to town the first time, he imagined himself doing what the evangelist was doing—preaching, inspiring, and leading others to faith in Christ. By the time the evangelist made his way back to the town a few years later, he'd already made up his mind: "I want to serve God and preach the gospel."

This is how my imagination runs wild sometimes. I imagine that Timothy, the young understudy of the apostle Paul, must have entered into the pastorate in a way similar to that. But the real point is that Timothy appeared to have been raised without his father's spiritual nurture and presence. This meant he was probably missing something he sorely needed—his father's affirmation. Maybe his father did affirm him, but there's no record of it in the Bible. I'm certain he received affirmation from his mother and his grandmother. They were his spiritual influences. And given the dedication and commitment he showed in his early ministerial development, I'd say those ladies did a tremendous job!

But Paul, at the sunset of his own ministry, gave Timothy what perhaps his father had not—what I theorize was swirling beneath the surface of Timothy's faith and his faithfulness. Life in ministry can be taxing and overwhelming. I know that from experience. Energy and perspective can be drained quickly, leaving you dazed, disheartened, and disillusioned. In 2 Timothy 1:3-8 and 3:10, Paul pours the refreshing spring waters of affirmation on a young minister who is worn and weary from the battle of dealing with spiritual opposition, the needs of people, exhaustion, discouragement, and its twin brother fear.

Paul reminded Timothy how grateful he was for him, that he prayed for him daily, and how much he looked forward to their reconnecting someday. He affirmed the genuineness of Timothy's faith. (Don't we need somebody who can see right through our weaknesses and fears and our worst days and affirm the *real good* in us?) Paul wouldn't let a discouraged Timothy lose sight of who he really was—genuine and authentic even though disillusioned. Paul affirmed Timothy's value and giftedness. He refused to let Timothy settle for second or anything less than his God-given potential.

You see, Timothy had lain down his spiritual gift and perhaps was ready to walk away from the work. I call it being annoyed by your anointing. Just because you're doing what God designed and saved you to do doesn't mean there won't be seasons when the weight feels like too much to carry. Real-life challenges will do that to anyone. It seems to happen especially to men. Timothy's flame for his work had blown out. His passion had fizzled. The thrill was gone, as BB King use to say. But Paul poured on what he needed— words of affirmation—to remind Timothy that his best days were ahead of him … that he had what it takes. For "God has not given us a spirit of fear, but of power and of love and of a sound mind" (1 Timothy 1:7).

> *If God the Father wouldn't let God the Son begin His magnum opus (great work) without affirmation, why let your son, your husband, or your students begin the day or a big assignment without it?*

The affirmations that Timothy's mother and grandmother had likely poured into his life were needed all the more as Timothy grew into manhood and began to take on his life's vocation. In other words, we men don't outgrow our need for affirmation, no matter how old we get, how successful we become, or how strong we appear to be. Our need for the nourishment of affirmation never dies. Like the food that fuels us with energy for life's demands and activities, so is affirmation.

Ladies, please don't miss this. The men who mean the most to you are never going to outgrow the positive impact of positive words and positive feedback. As I write this, I just celebrated my fifty-second birthday. I'm grayer than I've ever been and, of course, older than I've ever been. I'm an independent, entrepreneurial, highly motivated type. God has blessed my life, my pursuits, and my ministry beyond anything I ever imagined. And I still gain energy and encouragement when Sheri tells me how much my work blesses her and how much she believes in me.

It doesn't mean you have to be the only one affirming the men who mean the most to you. But it does mean that if you have a significant place in his life as his wife, his big sister, or his "auntie," etc., you should be one of his affirmers. It doesn't mean that he doesn't need someone in his life to challenge him with truth he may need to hear. It just means that if your relationship with him gives you the green light to challenge him, you should use the same green light to affirm him. I know I speak for many of my brothers: We need it.

The Wisdom of Affirmation

Is the need for affirmation just a weakness that people should get over? Is there something wrong with you if you need people to affirm you? Shouldn't we be able to get through life without needing people to approve of us? To be sure, requiring that all of our affirmation be found in people before we can move forward in life with confidence is not healthy. Neither is it God's intention.

No one can provide all the affirmation we need apart from God. But needing *it* is not necessarily *neediness*. In His infinite wisdom, God has built into us the capacity to be and do our best when the wind of affirmation is regularly blown beneath our wings.

One of the most profound pictures of God's relationship with Himself in the Trinity is seen at Jesus' baptism. In Matthew 3:13-17, God the Father affirmed God the Son, and God the Holy Spirit landed gently upon Him, preparing the Son for the launch of His public ministry:

> Then Jesus came from Galilee to John at the Jordan to be baptized by him. And John tried to prevent Him, saying, "I need to be baptized by You, and are You coming to me?"
>
> But Jesus answered and said to him, "Permit it to be so now, for thus it is fitting for us to fulfill all righteousness." Then he allowed Him.
>
> When He had been baptized, Jesus came up immediately from the water; and behold, the heavens were opened to Him, and He saw the Spirit of God descending like a dove and alighting upon Him. And suddenly a voice came from heaven, saying, "This is My beloved Son, in whom I am well pleased."

The particular statement that has long grabbed my attention is the last sentence in the chapter. Do you see it? *"This is my beloved Son ... "* Now look closely: *"... in whom I am well pleased."*

It strikes me as both strange and amazing that God the Father chose His words toward the Son so specifically ... so meaningfully. In His infinite wisdom, God the Father knew the enormity of the Son's mission—"to seek and to save the lost." With His perfect wisdom, God the Father chose his words: "in whom I am well pleased." If those are not words of affirmation, I don't know what they are. The Father affirmed the Son—even before the Son had done a single ministerial miracle of healing, deliverance, forgiveness, or saving one single person.

Write it on the white board of your memory in the most legible ink you can find: The Father's affirmation came *before* the Son entered the wilderness where He was tried in the fire of the devil's temptations. We might say, "before all hell broke loose in His life." Before the demands of His work were fully upon Him, before the attacks of the devil came for Him, and before He accomplished any victories, God the Father affirmed the Son.

Therein lies the wisdom of affirmation. Give it *before* it's needed. Give it *before* it's earned. Give it because it's needed. Give it to set the tone. "You're the man for the job. You've got this. I know the work is in good hands with you. God is going to show up for you and use you. I'm cheering for you!" God the Father conveyed His pleasure and full approval of the Son. He sanctioned the man and the mission, confirming Jesus to be the solution to humanity's biggest problem: sin. There are some jobs you don't want to have to begin until you know that someone believes in you.

Can you see the wisdom, ladies? If God the Father wouldn't let God the Son begin His *magnum opus* (great work) without affirmation, why let your son, your husband, or your students begin the day or a big assignment without it? How much more spiritual attack could they face with faith if their day began with a word of affirmation? How much more could they accomplish in their work and toward their dreams with your affirmation? How much better could they battle discouragement, fear, uncertainty, and second-guessing themselves with the wisdom of your affirming words?

If affirmation is wisdom, then my wife is a very wise woman. More than anyone else I can think of, she has built up my confidence as a visionary and leader. Her affirming words and willingness to see more in me than sometimes I saw in myself has changed the trajectory of my life. Sometimes it's not even her words; it's her actions.

I'll never forget the days when we began planting Messiah Community Church in our family room. It was the toughest year of my life. I was serving as the chaplain of the Baltimore Ravens in a full-time capacity while developing a launch team for the church. The only times we could meet with our launch team was on Sunday mornings during the off-season or Sunday evenings during the football season. Just thinking about the workload now is making me tired. There were several times during the season of launch meetings in our home that I just wanted to quit. The vision had great value, but the cost had to be counted weekly. It was extraordinary! To say the least, the cost was high—to my children, to the décor in our home, to the safety of our family (Sometimes really strange people are attracted to new church plants!), and to my spiritual well-being.

Some Saturday nights I went to bed depressed and unenthused about the next day's gathering. I recall telling Sheri on more than one occasion, "This is the last Sunday. I can't do this anymore." My wife would simply listen to my groans, get up early in the morning, pray fervently to God, then go to the market to buy fresh fruit, coffee, and donuts for our team. Not once can I remember her saying, "Yeah, I agree. I knew that when we first started. This is ridiculous. What's wrong with you, Rod? Nobody does this insanity!" She simply acted in wisdom toward my dream, affirming the vision God had placed in my heart. Now thirteen years, hundreds of families, and two properties later, the vision is more alive than ever. I have God to thank for wisely putting a woman of wisdom by my side to affirm me before anything significant had ever happened with the ministry we call *Messiah*.

The Ways of Affirmation

I like to think of affirmation as having personality. In other words, it has ways about it. Much like people and living creatures, affirmation seems to me to have particular qualities that characterize it. The very nature of the word suggests it has positive attributes. I don't know if it's because I speak, preach, write, and coach for a living, but I love discovering the meaning of words and observing their impact on people. On every one of my smart devices, I have the app called *Dictionary.com*. I don't write a talk, sermon, article, or book without it.

So quite naturally, I looked up the word *affirmation*. Here's what I found: "from the Latin *affirmare* … to make steady, to strengthen, to corroborate or make more certain, to make firm." Wow! Forgive me for geeking out, but I just love the power of words. Before I began writing this chapter, I had a hunch about the word. I suspected it had to have positive and progressive attributes. The way of affirmation is that it leaves people stronger, more certain, and steadier.

So, ladies, if you're wondering how to affirm the guy who needs your affirmations, here are some suggestions. First, communicate in ways and do things that inspire forward movement and positive thinking. It's easy to knock the life out of someone with our words. It takes intentional thought to give life with our words. "Life and death are in the power of the tongue" says Proverbs 18:21. And "The tongue of the wise promotes health," says Proverbs 12:18. In other words, we get to choose how we use our tongues toward others. In our tongues is the potential to make people come alive and the potential to snuff the life out of them. That would be murder! Ladies, did you know you have so much power in you?

I recently witnessed a very attractive woman single-tonguedly destroy her marriage and nearly destroy her husband. I just made up that word, because she didn't do it with her hands. She did it with her words. It wasn't that she didn't love God. It wasn't that she didn't post Bible verses from her YouVersion Bible app. She even served in her local church. But from the time their relationship began until the divorce, her husband lamented that she constantly tore him down with her words. I hesitated to believe he was representing her tongue accurately. I couldn't imagine someone who practiced so many of the "right" things in their faith saying some of the things I was told she said to him. And then one day, in the middle of a heated argument, he dialed my number while they were squabbling and set his phone down. I can't repeat the unbelievable barrage of damaging words I heard, but I can tell you, it made my jaw hit the floor. Even having been an NFL chaplain, I never heard language like that even in a locker room or on the sideline. Sadly, she never embraced this truth: "A wholesome tongue is a tree of life, / But perverseness in it breaks the spirit" (Proverbs 15:4).

In contrast to the story of the couple I shared above, the ways of affirmation move people forward, make life-giving deposits, encourage progress, and make positive declarations. Ladies, I know you can give life when you speak, even when you have to be critical or hold him accountable. God has placed the potential in you. All you have to do is access it. It takes a little bit of skill, a little bit of thought, a little bit of art, and a growing heart for God.

The prophet Isaiah is one of my Bible heroes. I look up to him in large part because of his brutal honesty … about his own shortcoming. One day he had a vision of God sitting on His throne with angels flying above, crying out to one another, "Holy, holy, holy is the LORD of hosts; The whole earth is full of His glory!" That would have shaken anyone to the core. I'm not sure how I would have reacted to such a vision, but Scripture gives us Isaiah's immediate reaction. He cried out in despair, "Woe is me, for I am undone!" Isaiah thought he was going to die right there, right then because the moment was so overwhelming. As I looked more closely at Isaiah 6:1-10, what struck me was the reason he thought he was going to die. Isaiah thought this was the end for him because he had a potty-mouth: "Because I am a man of unclean lips …."

Whether we men say it or not, we long to be affirmed. We need it. We thrive on it. Many of us are deprived of its very oxygen in our lives. We're panting with thirst for it and deprived of the nourishment it feeds our souls.

It was Isaiah's heart for God that made him want to watch his mouth so God could use him as His spokesperson. When he saw God for whom He is, Isaiah wanted to do better with his words, so He allowed one of the angels to wash out his mouth. Actually, The angel scorched his tongue with a glowing-hot piece of stone. Ouch!!! It hurts just to think about it. The point is this: In order to walk in the ways of affirmation, we first have to be open to a painful cleansing of our tongues. After the angel burned Isaiah's tongue, God released him to speak on His behalf. But it all began with Isaiah's honesty and his heart for God.

Isaiah's burning hot coal encounter changed his life and his lips, his speech tactics and his tongue. The prophet with the potty-mouth grew into a world-changer for God. Here's the evidence: "The LORD God has given me / The tongue of the learned, / That I should know how to speak / A word in season to him who is weary." (Isaiah 50:4). In essence, Isaiah learned how to use his tongue to lift up and encourage—to affirm—the weary. How? He allowed God to disciple his tongue. He learned to listen to God before he opened his mouth. As we preachers like to say to one another, "That'll preach!"

Ladies, walking in the ways of affirmation toward the men who matter most to you requires a certain way of thinking, a touch of art, and some skill. The process begins with growing your heart for God by being available to hear from Him. The potty-mouthed prophet was daily transformed: "He awakens Me morning by morning, He awakens my ear / To hear as the learned. The LORD God has opened my My ear; / And I was not rebellious, / Nor did I turn away."

Allowing God to disciple your tongue, ladies, will make you a communicator who chooses her words wisely, times them precisely, and delivers them effectively. Isaiah was able to say that God gave him a new tongue—the tongue of the learned. The tongue of the learned is the tongue of someone who waits for God to make clear what to say, when to say it, and how to say it, so the listener can go from being weary, discouraged, and exhausted to feeling lifted, encouraged, and yes, affirmed. Get ready, my sisters, to see the men you love go to another level because of your powerful, affirming words in their lives!

Chapter 1 Reflections:

1. Whether we men say it or not, we long to be affirmed. We need it. We thrive on it. Many of us are deprived of its very oxygen in our lives. We're panting with thirst for it and deprived of the nourishment it feeds our souls.

2. If God the Father wouldn't let God the Son begin His *magnum opus* (great work) without affirmation, why let your son, your husband, or your students begin the day or a big assignment without it?

3. Ladies, walking in the ways of affirmation toward the men who matter

most to you requires a certain way of thinking, a touch of art, and some skill. The process begins with growing your heart for God by being available to hear from Him.

2

Pray for Him:
Change Things Behind The Scenes

I am thoroughly convinced that the most powerful tool (and weapon) at anyone's disposal is prayer. But I have a personal bias: I think women, especially mothers, have a unique audience with God. When a godly woman makes requests of the Almighty God on a son's, father's, or husband's behalf, things change. Demons tremble. Mountains move. Doors open. Destructive vices lose their grip. Behind the scenes of his life, things begin to shift. He may not even know why, especially if you never told him you were praying for him. Things just begin to change. No devil in Hell can succeed in his attacks against the guy who has the force of a godly woman's prayers behind him.

Ladies, sometimes you can't talk a man into change. You can't convince him against his will—even when the thing you're trying to convince him of is good for him. But your prayers have the ability to "turn on the lights" for him when he can't see a danger ahead. Your prayers help combat the discouragements of life that may come against him. Your prayers get him through a tough day of meetings, pressures, stresses, and decisions. Your prayers lift him from the pits of despair and usher him to a higher, more joy-filled dimension of life—closer to the God who loves him and has great things in store for him. You don't have to tell him you're praying for him. Just do it and watch change happen!

Prayer: The Indispensable Weapon (Ephesians 6:18-19)
I'm not one of those preachers to whom messages come easy. I study faithfully, make earnest efforts to "pray without ceasing," and put in the time needed to craft effective sermons filled with biblical truth. But preaching and pastoring are harder work than anyone ever told me they would be.

Two nights ago, I was having a fit trying to synthesize my notes from the week's study and preparation. My wife posed her usual Saturday afternoon question: "How is your sermon for tomorrow coming along?" I just looked at her with that look that says, "What sermon?" The study portion was complete, and I've learned that prayer (and sleep) do more for me than trying to press out an outline for teaching and preaching. So I prayed and went to bed. When I awoke, my brain was swimming in a sea of new insights from God concerning His kingdom and His purpose for families. All Sheri said was, "I'm praying for you."

I can't explain it any other way. I just know that when my wife prays for me, heaven moves. She has a connection with God that I only wish I had. I know that a rested brain is one of God's kindest gifts and solutions for solving problems. But that woman's prayers often go far beyond my rested brain and beyond my personal prayers. I gain clarity, calm, and confidence because of her connection to God. That's all the more reason for me to love and appreciate her. I can't imagine my life or my ministry without her covering me and my efforts with her prayers.

Prayer is indispensable because everyone needs prayer. It's something that no one can do without. It gives everyone the opportunity to see his or her life get better. Having someone talk to God on your behalf about your biggest fears, challenges, questions, and quests is a game-changer. Having someone access the power of heaven and a God who can move mountains on another's behalf makes prayer something no one can live without.

Unfortunately, not everyone knows the value and power of prayer. And not everyone has access to God in prayer. Those are not indictments or judgments; they're simply realities. Until a person has begun a relationship with God through faith in Jesus, the Bible is clear that he or she cannot experience the privilege of intimate and confident prayer. Jesus told His disciples, "Until now, you have not asked anything in my name. Ask, and you will receive, that your joy may be full" (John 16:24). Jesus was extending to His disciples a new level of privilege and access to God the Father. They were, because of their faith in Jesus, invited to use His powerful name as their "calling card" with the Father.

The writer of Hebrews saw prayer as a unique privilege granted to those who have Jesus as their High Priest—the one who has gone to God on their behalf and offered the sacrifice of His life for their sin. And He knew that what could be obtained through prayer was vital to our human needs: "Let us therefore come boldly to the throne of grace, that we may obtain mercy and find grace to help in time of need" (Hebrews 4:14-16). Have you ever seen a person in trouble, in over their heads in life, and facing the challenge of a lifetime? That person needs what can only be obtained in prayer: sympathy from a God who cares deeply, empathy from a God who has placed Himself in man's shoes, favor (another word for grace) from a God who can put us at the front of the line, and compassionate mercy that only God can give us in a world that can be brutally cold.

That's the *indispensable* nature of prayer. But prayer is also a powerful weapon that can be wielded to defeat dark and destructive forces for the good and help of others. The Bible describes in factual terms—not metaphors, figures of speech, or similes, but in day-to-day reality—the existence of the Devil and his workforce called demons. They have one collective agenda under the Devil's headship: "to kill, to steal, and to destroy" (John 10:10). Prayer, aligned with biblical truth, is the primary weapon we have for undoing Satan's plans against us and the people we care about.

Prayer, the ability to communicate with God, receive His directions, and request His assistance, positions everyday people like you and me to experience victory over "our adversary the devil" who is out to devour people (1 Peter 5:8). Whenever someone is out to devour us, that's not a good thing. And when someone is out to devour the men you care about, it's exponentially bad. *Devour* means to *drink down, swallow up, or gulp entirely.* When Satan sets his sights on your husband, son, brother, or friend, he pulls out all the stops. He plays by no rules, and there is no referee calling him back to his corner so his victim can regain strength. Only God has the power to shut down a Satanic, demonic attack.

That makes prayer a weapon in the hands of a woman who embraces a call from God to cover a man in her life. Prayer neutralizes the enemy's weapons. It unleashes powerful angelic forces against his army in the unseen realm. It is not hindered by geography, time, culture, circumstance, or any other would-be obstacle. Prayer, as a spiritual weapon is powerful! As Paul said,

For though we walk in the flesh, we do not war according to the flesh. For the weapons of our warfare are not carnal but mighty in God for pulling down strongholds, casting down arguments and every high thing that exalts itself against the knowledge of God, bringing every thought into captivity to the obedience of Christ, and being ready to punish all disobedience when your obedience is fulfilled. (2 Corinthians 10:3-6)

Prayer is a weapon that Satan is powerless to defeat. Just imagine what is possible in a man's life when you use it!

Prayer: The Silent Shaper (Proverbs 22:19)

What if you could change someone's mind, influence his decisions, or introduce an alternative perspective … without ever saying a word to them? What if you could calm a storm of anger raging in your man and keep him from taking vengeful action that would harm his future and the life of someone else? What if you could positively influence a man to see himself the way God sees him rather than continuing to see himself through a lens that robs him of value and esteem? You would be a very powerful person. Having that ability would make you someone who can shape the course or direction of a man's life. That's extraordinary influence!

Words are by nature powerful, but there are certain cases in which their power is ineffective—even when they're well-meaning. That's not to say words ought never to be used. But it is wise to know when words may not be useful and when they have reached their limit in a man's ears. On a very human level, words can be limited sometimes by the fact that a man may just not want to hear them. Sometimes, as a man, my mind is made up and I don't want it to be changed. So trying to talk me into or out of something is pointless. Sometimes, I just want to feel that the decision to change my mind came from me. (Hint, hint.) Call me egotistical, but sometimes that's just the way it is.

Proverbs 21:1 says, "The king's heart is in the hand of the Lord, / Like the rivers of water; He turns it wherever He wishes." In essence, the writer is giving us the key to silently shaping a man's thought processes, decisions, and even his feelings about a matter. It's not manipulation that gets things done in and through a man. It's the powerful influence of prayer.

Ladies, if you want to see your man make decisions that are good for him, his family, and his future … If you want to see him check his emotions before something irreversibly negative happens, here is your key: Go to the person who has the "Big Key" to his heart. Go to God. Your prayers to God convey your trust in God more than your trust in your own ability to get a man to do something. When you go to God, you're surrendering (or will eventually surrender) your well-intended agenda or timing. That man's heart, because he's designed to be a leader/influencer, is in the Lord's hands, and He can point it in any direction He desires. God has the power to do that.

> *When a godly woman makes requests of the Almighty God on a son's, father's, or husband's behalf, things change. Demons tremble. Mountains move. Doors open. Destructive vices lose their grip. Behind the scenes of his life, things begin to shift.*

There have been times when my wife clearly did not like the decision I was making. Whether in my anger, folly, fogginess, or immaturity, she has often been able to sense danger ahead if my leadership in a matter was not abated. I now know when I'm about to hit a wall, because rather than give me all the reasons why she thinks I should or should not move in a particular direction, she gets that look on her face. It's hard to describe, but I know it when I see it. It simply says, "Okay. I'll be praying, because you sound like you have just lost your mind, Roderick Lorenzo Hairston." (I always know I'm in trouble when I feel that she's thinking my full, legal name!) Then she smiles and says, "Let me know if you change your mind."

Prayer: The Eye Opener (2 Kings 6:8-23)

It doesn't matter how intelligent, talented, or celebrated a person may be. If you cannot see, you cannot see. In other words, blindness, or if you will, blind spots, are not easily overcome. Everyone has them. Ladies, the men in your lives have blind spots, and you probably know what they are. The only problem is that knowing someone's blind spot doesn't mean you can make them see what they can't see. Blind spots are not simply what we can't see about ourselves. Blind spots may also be what we can't see outside ourselves or within ourselves. For example, we may not detect the danger ahead of us. We may have a perpetual attitude of defeatism and not realize it. We may lack confidence and fail to realize how capable we are and what experiences and resources we have at our disposal.

There are some things we'll never see and some perspectives we may never gain apart from having our literal and proverbial eyes opened through prayer. One of my all-time favorite passages in the Bible is the story of the prophet Elisha who had deeply irritated the Syrian King, Ben-Hadad (2 Kings 4:8-23). While the Syrian king had been plotting to attack Israel and bring down God's people and their king, the prophet of Israel gave to Israel's king insight into the enemy's plans, which he had received through divine revelation. Elisha could see what no one else could see, and as a result the people of Israel were protected. The frustrated and enraged Ben-Hadad wanted to know who was leaking his plans and strategies to his enemies.

Having learned that Elisha, the man of God, was giving insights to the king of Israel, making it impossible for Ben-Hadad to successfully attack and destroy God's people, "he sent horses and chariots and a great army" (2 Kings 6:14) to deal with Elisha. He considered Elisha a snitch who must be killed. As the Syrian army approached the city early one morning to surround it, Elisha's servant saw them in the distance and panicked. He said, "Alas my master! What shall we do?" Elisha gave him encouragement: "Do not fear, for those who are with us are more than those who are with them" (v. 16). "Okay, that all sounds good, but what are you smoking, my master Elisha? More with us? There's nobody here but you and me. And we're about to lose our lives!" Can't you hear Elisha's servant in panic mode?

Elisha's servant couldn't see what Elisha was able to see using his spiritual eyes. Elisha could see invisible angelic forces of heaven surrounding the forces of the Syrian king. I hear what you're thinking: "Who in the world sees angels? I thought they were invisible." Usually they are invisible, but when you have a connection to God as Elisha did, God allows you to see things. And even if you can't see them, you can do for the man in your life what Elisha did for his servant: he prayed, "LORD, I pray, open his eyes that he may see" (v. 17). And that's exactly what God did. God opened the servant's eyes so he could see that the army fighting for him and Elisha was bigger with more fire-power than the one that had come to destroy them. I'm typing with goose bumps because this blows my mind! If I can't see God's provision, it's because my perspective gets hijacked by the problem I can see. If I can't see, I need to have my eyes opened so I can see the situation the way God sees it. I need to see God's support system that He has put in place for my good.

Ladies, a simple prayer for the man you care about could change everything: "LORD, I pray that You will open his eyes that he may see." Prayer commences an eye-opening experience. It opens your own eyes as much as it opens those of the one you're praying for. Prayer will keep your guy from panicking. It'll keep him from being consumed with fear and overwhelmed by responsibilities. It'll keep him from traveling a path of defeatism and grant him the revelation that God has surrounded his enemies. Pray that God will open his eyes so he'll know exactly who God says he is and what God says he has. Pray for eyes of clarity when people who could destroy him come into his life like wolves in sheep's clothing, disguised as angels of light. Pray that your man will have an eye-opening experience with God and that he'll never see the same … or be the same.

Prayer: The Determiner of Destiny (Exodus 17:1-23)
The Israelites were barely out of Egypt and filled with uncertainty concerning their destiny. Who of us cannot relate to that dilemma—out of a bad situation but uncertain about the next steps or the final destination? Israel's enemy, as expected, took full advantage of their vulnerability. Their first real "opposition" was having to face extreme thirst at a place called Rephidim. There was no water anywhere in sight, and the people complained about Moses' sense of direction as a leader. They concluded that the LORD was not with them (Exodus 17:1-7). No water to drink in the desert and feeling deserted by the God who came to deliver them led them to believe they had no destiny.

Opposition to Israel's destiny escalated to another level at Rephidim when the Amalekite army came against Moses and the newly delivered Israelites. Moses sent his assistant, Joshua, out to lead the neophyte troops in battle, while Moses, Aaron, and Hur climbed to the top of the hill to oversee the battle with prayer. Moses climbed the hill with the symbol of his leadership and spiritual authority—the rod of his God—in hand. His staff symbolized his access to God and the power of God for his role as Israel's shepherd. With it he could work miracles, or with it he could punish wolves who would attack the flock.

As the battle with Amalek ensued, Moses, positioned on the hilltop, held up his hands with his staff in one of them. When he became tired and his hands lowered, his troops suffered loss. Over the course of the battle, Moses' hands grew *heavy*. What a picture of the fight for destiny against our enemies! It reminds us that prayer is hard work because so much is at stake. To keep the leader's hands up so he could pray in the power of God with his staff lifted in the desire for victory, Aaron and Hur placed a rock under Moses so he could sit. And while he sat with his hands lifted, they each supported his hands on either side. In the end, Joshua and the Israelite army were able to defeat the Amalekites. They did so because Moses prayed with the support of Aaron and Hur.

Ladies, as my friend Pastor Keith Battle says, "every man needs an Aaron and a *Her* in his life." He needs someone lifting up his arms with prayer so his destiny is not waylaid by foul "Amalekites"—i.e., those assigned by the devil to block the way and to wipe out God's people, keeping them from progressing toward their destiny.

Chapter 2 Reflections:

1. When a godly woman makes requests of the Almighty God on a son's, father's, or husband's behalf, things change. Demons tremble. Mountains move. Doors open. Destructive vices lose their grip. Behind the scenes of his life, things begin to shift.

2. Prayer is indispensable because everyone needs prayer. It's something that no one can do without. It gives everyone the opportunity to see his or her life get better. Having someone talk to God on your behalf about your biggest fears, challenges, questions, and quests is a game changer.

3. Ladies, if you want to see your man make decisions that are good for

him, his family, and his future … If you want to see him check his emotions before something irreversibly negative happens, here is your key: Go to the person who has the "Big Key" to his heart. Go to God.

3

Respect Him:
Give Him Something He Can Feel

Aretha Franklin said it! "R-E-S-P-E-C-T ... Find out what it means to me."
Then she dropped another hit filled with practical wisdom when it comes to
men. She said, *"I'm givin' him something he can feel!"* You have to know
the song and feel the weight of soul that only The Queen of Soul could've
put into it.

I know Aretha had something else—something a little more sensual—
in mind, and we'll get to that later in the book. But respect is definitely
something a man can feel. It's not merely something to be heard with words.
Respect is not a cerebral exercise in contemplation. Respect is something
we feel. And we feel it deeply—down to the core of our being, down deep
in our souls. We feel it when it's there. And believe me, we feel it when
it's not there. We can absolutely feel when we are treated and regarded as
someone worthy and weighty. Men feel respect.

We know when we're respected, and we know when we're not
respected. Asking a man whether he can tell if someone respects him is
like asking him whether he can tell night from day, hot from cold, white
from black. We know it instinctively. As I said, we feel it. To express your
love to a man is cool. But respect is the game-changer for men. He knows
you love him if he knows you respect him. In fact, the woman who shows
a man the most respect wins. It means that much to a man.

I'm well aware that this is a point in the book where I risk losing a
lot of readers. For a moment our conversation about women and men may
feel a little one-sided. Trust me. That's neither my thought process nor
my intention. I have a very strong commitment to the value, respect, and
dignity of women. That's why my first book was called *Cover Her.*

Oftentimes when there's a discussion about women respecting men,
questions come up that usually go something like this: "Why should I have

to respect him … because he's a man? What if he hasn't earned my respect? After all, if he wants respect, he should handle his responsibilities like a man and stop acting like an adolescent. When is he going to grow up? When he does, I'll respect him." This line of questioning and reasoning often goes on, usually quite legitimately and understandably. And almost always, passionately and emphatically. Much of this attitude often reflected by women, men in our culture have brought upon ourselves.

With the widening voice and awareness the #MeToo movement is bringing to the world, respect from women toward men may be at an all-time low in society. And in many ways, it makes absolute sense. I thank God for the awareness #MeToo is bringing to the long history of physical and sexual abuse, harassment, and foul treatment women of all ages have suffered at the hands of and under the power of men. Many men have dropped the ball of our responsibilities to women and society. Much worse, we've straight-up thrown the ball away in many cases. We've harmed and hurt the women we are designed to cover. We've abandoned our children for the office, the golf course, and the ballpark. We've grabbed our beers, gaming consoles, and remote controls and checked out of the fight for our families and others who need our strength. If respect is earned, a lot of men are in deep, deep trouble!

> *God designed men in such a way that respect is core to our identity. Even as young boys, we grope for it among our peers. As we grow into our teen and adult years, we gain respect principally through our work and our ability to produce a living. How well we do our craft, face the challenges that come with it, and earn from it are a matter of respect for men.*

The Heart of Respect

So what do we do with the principle found in Ephesians 5:33? "Nevertheless let each one of you in particular love his own wife as himself, and *let the wife see that she respects her husband*" (italics mine). We have a real dilemma on our hands. Does the call for respect extend beyond the marriage relationship? Is there some cultural nuance behind the apostle

Paul's admonition that makes the verse irrelevant to our day and time? Why is *respect* the single issue in Paul's teaching in the wife-to-husband, woman-to-man dynamic? I don't have answers to all of those questions, but I'd like to offer my humble take.

You may have been exposed to ridiculously male-dominant interpretations of the Bible's views on women. If so, I hope you'll give me an opportunity to share from a more balanced perspective. If after humoring me, you still don't agree, I certainly won't be offended. I really do understand. But please assume my intentions are honorable as I present my understanding of Scripture on the matter. I hope you will find it helpful.

Respect is an expression of relationship and a key to any healthy relationship. No relationship can thrive where there is not mutual respect. The respect aspect of Ephesians 5:33 does not imply a one-way street, as if women are to respect men but men have no obligation to show respect to women. Quite the opposite is true. A husband's love for his wife strongly implies treating her with respect as his equal in the relationship. As Genesis makes clear, Eve was created in the image of God just as Adam was. That makes her equally valuable, dignified, and worthy of respect.

Paul's point is simply this: A woman thrives when she experiences sacrificial, covering love from her husband—the kind of love that is unconditional and treats her with respect. And a husband thrives when he experiences, from his wife, deep regard for his strengths, abilities, and accomplishments. The broader principle that applies to relationships between women and men in general goes something like this: Men, treat her with the value God has given her; she is not an object nor is she a lesser being. Esteem her and dignify her as your equal, who is capable and inherently valuable. Ladies, acknowledge that God put inside of him the potential to lead, to protect, and to provide. He may not be fully living up to his potential, but it is in there. If you don't see him living up to it, affirm and acknowledge any strengths, abilities, and accomplishments you see him living out positively. What gets celebrated gets repeated. That's the heart of respect.

Ephesians 5:33b speaks to a deep need in men—something I believe was lost in Genesis 3:17-19 when Adam failed in his leadership assignment. Eve entered the garden story later than Adam and may not have received directly all of God's warnings about sin. Rather than protect Eve from the deception of Satan, Adam sat passively. He was near Eve when Satan worked to twist her perspective, making her believe God didn't have her best interest in mind. What's worse, rather than fight to protect her, he filled his belly with the forbidden fruit. Adam took the path of least resistance and the path of maximum pleasure. He took the couch-potato route. He treated God's command to guard the garden and his wife carelessly and selfishly. I'm still mad at Adam! He let a snake weasel his way in and mess up the blessed harmony he and Eve had with God. He forfeited the sweat-free provision and abundant supply of the garden. He invited contention … all because he refused to confront the issues, namely the devil's deception and his own appetite. Adam shrunk back from unavoidable conflict—the kind of stuff life is made of and which men must confront straight ahead.

Adam lost Eve's respect in that moment, in my opinion. And that has been the lynchpin matter between men and women ever since. Eve's actions came with consequences particular to her as a woman—difficulty in childbirth, having to clamor for the attention and affection of her husband, and having to always watch her back against attacks launched by Satan—i.e., enmity between her and Satan (Genesis 3:15). But Adam's failure resulted in consequences they'd both have to suffer the rest of their earthly lives—hard, unproductive ground to till and sow, painful thorns and useless thistles to contend with all their lives, limited edible vegetation, and a sweaty and toilsome approach to work and provision in life. Adam's passivity caused their Edenic existence to become a total grind.

It's no wonder Eve lost respect for Adam. He surrendered his spine to a spineless snake and left his woman vulnerable to his lies. These failures would become the proving grounds of the man's masculinity and respectability. In other words, will he have the courage to protect against predators? Will he speak the truth in the face of deception? Will he act against his own comfort for a woman's good? A woman's ultimate evaluation of a man should come down to this: Is he respectable?

Since the garden of Eden, respect has become the thing every "Adam Junior" has found himself longing for, even fighting for. There is not room enough in this book to tell you all the false and illegitimate ways men have pursued respectability, but here are a few: sexual conquest, financial status,

Cover Him

political power, social status, material possessions, luxury and comforts, educational accomplishment, and physical stature. Each of these has legitimate expressions when obtained the right way and used for the good of others and the glory of God. But ever since Adam, we Adam Juniors have struggled to keep things in perspective. Only in Christ do we have any chance of getting it right. The struggle for respect is real.

So what should you, as a woman, do with these insights? How do they apply across the spectrum of relationships between women and men?

A Legacy of Disrespect

After nearly twenty year of marriage, the fairy tale was becoming a draining nightmare. Jason had lost interest in sexual intimacy, and Karen's resentment and feelings of rejection had her contemplating her options. The children were excelling academically, athletically, and socially, but something was missing at home. Jason and Karen admitted to me several times that things were not well and that they were at wits end.

Both of them hated the thought of divorce. They'd seen the drama and the pain it caused in families when their own parents divorced. But the idea of continuing in a cold, touchless, loveless, sexless, and "let's-just-pay-the-bills" life together had Karen drinking more and Jason working longer hours. The cycles of anger, resentment, and silence were taking a toll on them both and on their amazing kids.

At the heart of their relational distance was the lack of respect Jason had been feeling since day-one of their marriage. The snowball of disrespect had grown slowly and steadily until it became an avalanche barreling down the mountain. To Jason, it seemed that history was repeating itself. He'd grown up in a home where his mother had no respect for his father. She abandoned her husband, along with Jason and his older brother. Jason loved his mom, but he seldom, if ever, spoke about the pain her leaving caused him. He'd seen the disrespect his father endured. And he felt it. How could the woman who'd given birth to him and his brother just pack up and walk out, showing up mostly just for big occasions?

Karen also brought to the marriage baggage from her past. She was the offspring of a relationship of sexual convenience. Her father acknowledged her but was not relationally invested with her. After he completed his medical studies and began his practice in another state, she rarely saw him—except when he came to town with his new wife and their two daughters. While his new family was raised with all the benefits of a two-physician, two-income home, Karen's mother struggled to make ends meet. And Karen always felt like a stepchild to her own father, standing on the outside looking in at his *real* family. Worse yet, she felt that she never measured up and was always an inconvenience.

Jason and Karen were a storm waiting to happen! And the issue of respect was the eye of that storm. Not until they were well into their marriage did he realize how much disrespect he'd seen his mother direct toward his father. His father never lashed out in his pain with anger. He simply held everything in, enduring it all in silence as he nurtured his boys to become outstanding student athletes. Karen didn't realize how much she resented her father. How could she respect a man who hadn't invested in her relationally, financially, or emotionally? It's easy to see how Jason and Karen's pasts developed in them dangerous patterns of relating in their own marriage. Her words, tones, and responses often felt disrespectful to Jason. And his silence and emotional distance fueled an offshore storm until it became a full-blown hurricane that threatened to blow down twenty years of what they'd built together.

Thankfully, together they learned some valuable lessons about respect that reignited the flames of love and saved their marriage. Let me share with you a few of them.

Respect Is His Identity

In the housing project where I grew up, options for boyhood recreation were limitless. (They weren't always wholesome and safe. But if I mention some of them in this book, my mom will give me *the look*. She had no idea, so let's keep it that way.) One of the things we did in addition to the usual pick-up games of basketball, football, and soccer was jumping fences. Yes, we made a sport of jumping over chain-link fences throughout the housing project. For some reason, the standard three-foot fence varied in height in the hood.

Collections of boys from around the neighborhood would challenge one another as we went around to the various fences. Whoever didn't make it got his feelings and usually some part of his body hurt. Even as a kid I was a bookworm, but reading got no respect among my peers, and respect was the name of the game. Athletic ability was the measure. Can you jump? How high and how many? Even as boys of nine, ten, and eleven years of age, we sensed the need for respect. And if jumping meant big, oozing gashes in our legs and dirt on our faces, it was worth it. Those were the battle scars, and I have one on my left ankle to this day, to prove it. Ed, Tony, and Eric were always much better athletes than I was. But they respected my cerebral tendencies only because I jumped fences with them. The fences weren't the issue. They were simply a measure. They measured our juvenile courage, our willingness to face a challenge, and a legitimate attempt to scale that challenge.

As we grew into our puberty years and into our teens, we discovered another potential source of respect. Girls. Something shifted, as I now recall. We all went from laughing at the girls in our classes and avoiding them like the plague to secretly having "girlfriends." In our pre-girl years, recess had been a time for the boys to play our boy games—without the interruptive presence of girls. Our time at recess was so precious that there was no time to explain the rules to creatures who wouldn't understand them anyway. And besides that, girls were *icky*.

But something happened to us all by about tenth grade. Icky little girls were starting to *glow up* as my daughters call it. They suddenly went from the awkwardness of middle school with their pudginess, eyeglasses, and braces to OMG! It happened over a single summer—just that quickly. All the guys who had once prized our fence-jumping and cherished recess hour were now measuring our manhood by how good looking our girlfriends were ... and how many of them we had. Unfortunately, honesty compels me to tell you that many of us would measure our respectability by how many girls we were able to have sex with. We were fishing for respect, but our understanding of the matter was still quite juvenile, to say the least.

The point is this: God designed men in such a way that respect is core to our identity. Even as young boys, we grope for it among our peers. As we grow into our teen and adult years, we gain respect principally through our work and our ability to produce a living. How well we do our craft, face the challenges that come with it, and earn from it are a matter of respect for men.

When God placed Adam in the garden. He gave him a simple assignment: *"tend and keep it"* (Genesis 2:15 italics mine). Adam's responsibility was to work hard in and to watch protectively, over his garden. That's why when a man gets laid off from his job, something happens inside of him. His confidence takes a hit. And the longer he's out of work, the more negatively it affects him. In my former years as an NFL chaplain, the most challenging situation players faced was not being able to practice or compete due to injury. Most NFL players would rather compete injured with a shot of Toradol from the team physician than not be on the field with their teammates. The inability to participate in their craft often led to a diminished sense of worth and camaraderie with their teammates that sometimes took a toll on them. During times of prolonged injury, some struggled with heavy drinking, anger, depression, and even recreational drug use. There's something necessary about a man being able to get up, go to work, and produce income from it. It's a matter of respect.

The other way a man experiences respect is through his relationships with key women in his life. After God gave Adam work, He gave him Eve. She was the lady in his life. And ladies, this is where you come in. Whether you're his wife, significant other, sister, mom, or friend, your expressed respect toward him can have a profound impact on his psyche and on his life. (I'm not exaggerating.) He's better in every way when the women he loves respect and admire his hard work, excellence in his craft, and positive impact in the world. My wife, my daughters, my mom, my aunt Ruth, and my aunt Jean are those ladies in my life. Every time they speak well of my work as a pastor, my successes as a chaplain, my impact as an author, speaker, and coach, and my provision for my family, my steps get a little bit faster. I feel more sure of myself. My desire to do well goes to another level. Nothing is more powerful in my life than when Sheri, my bride of over twenty-seven years says, "I hope you know how much I respect you." It's game on then!

Respect Is His Love Language
My wife's love languages are multiple—touch, words of affirmation, and quality time. But the one that speaks loudest to her is acts of service. She feels loved when I actually speak love in language that she can hear. It took

me some time to figure it out. It thought that if I told her I loved her, she would know that I love her. And to some degree, she did. But she needed me to speak in ways that she could *hear*. She needed some actions that put my love on display. I discovered about twenty-five years into our marriage that when I hang her outdoor flags, give her a hand with household chores, help her move the furniture when she's decorating (and re-decorating ... and re-decorating ... and re-decorating) our home ... then she knows I love her.

What's true for my wife and for countless other women is true when it comes to respect for a man. Respect is a man's ultimate love language. Show him respect and he'll know for sure that you love him. Demonstrate respect and he will want to up his game. So what does respect for your man, your son, or any other man look like?

Respect Helps

When God created Eve, he gave her a distinct shape. The Bible says God *fashioned* her. God didn't make her as He did Adam, whom he formed from the dust of the ground. Eve He built. In other words, Eve was shaped in order to fit God's design of Adam. She was built to help him of whom God said, "it's not good for the man to be alone." Eve was God ingenious solution to Adam's lack of help and support in his life. Ladies, stay with me. Help is not a derogatory notion. It's the work of a God who knew just how to assign power to each of the sexes. Eve's power was in her ability and her necessity to Adam. Quite literally, he was incomplete without her. His maleness required her femaleness if he was going to stand a chance at fulfilling the assignment God had placed upon his life. Without Eve alongside him to help him, life for Adam would have been an eternal exercise in frustration. Her strengths were the missing pieces to his life's puzzle. He couldn't fulfill his destiny without her help.

Eve's assignment from God was to help Adam with the vision, plan, and calling God had placed on him. Her job, literally, was to encourage, inspire, and come alongside him so he could get the job done. Please don't overlook this very important assignment God has given to women. A man can only feel respected by you to the degree that you walk according to your design as a helper. So if you try to take over his work, try to dictate his work to him, speak ill of his work, or demean it, problems will arise and he will feel deeply disrespected.

A friend of mine who is a brilliant professor of mechanical engineering made this point very clear for me. After becoming frustrated with his work in academia, he left the university to pursue his real passion—repairing and restoring Mercedes-Benz cars of any era. You have to meet Sam to know that few people on the planet have his passion for these unique luxury cars. As he said to me one day, "Rod, I knew it was my passion and calling because the same energy I have at 6 AM in the shop, I have at 10 PM if I'm in the shop." I don't know if those hours are good for anyone on a regular basis. But that's not the point. The point is that Sam's wife didn't think much of her husband's passion. She couldn't understand why he would waste his time building a car repair business when he could better spend the time traveling with her to her medical meetings.

Sam's wife did everything she could to talk him out of his work and into traveling with her. In her mind, her work was more important and more valuable. What she missed was that Sam's sense of respect came from his passion for his work. The growing sense of disrespect in their marriage grew to the point where something had to give, so she filed for divorce. Because he would not leave his work, she left him.

The problem was that Sam's wife didn't realize that had she taken the posture of helping Sam grow the business, they could have thrived together and in their respective fields. Had she simply asked him how well he was moving toward his goals, she would have been helping him. Had she merely stopped by the shop to congratulate him on the progress, they might still be together. Had she found a way to celebrate him for taking the risk to follow his passion and for building a viable business out of what had been a side hobby, theirs would be a much better story. All Sam's wife had to do was find meaningful ways to help her Mr. Mercedes.

Ladies, every man who's important to you will benefit from your helpful spirit unless he is not on God's assignment for his life. Why? Because it is hard to help someone who has no idea where he's headed and what his assignment is from God. But even if he's not clear about his passion and direction, a simple and gentle gesture can help him. Buy him a book about what he seems to be good at, but don't lecture him. Let him know that you see something in him. If he had the gumption to write a business plan and attempt to start the business, support his attempts at entrepreneurship. Sitting on the sideline and griping at him or to your friends—"Girl, he's talking about starting a business. I told him he needs to get a job because he knows nothing about business"—will not help him.

Respect Builds Up

I've heard too many women tell their girlfriends how incompetent, clumsy, and clueless their men are. What's worse, I've heard from too many men how their wives dressed them down verbally: "You're such a punk. You do nothing around here. I don't know why I married you. Why can't you make more money? When you grow up, I'll be happy to give you some sex." I imagine she may feel justified in blasting him with her words. It's possible she could even be right in her descriptions of him. But one thing's for sure; she will never change him for the better with that kind of verbal assault and tongue-lashing.

King Lemuel, the writer of Proverbs 31, was taught by his mother that, "When she [a woman of noble character] speaks, her words are wise, and she gives instructions with kindness" (Proverbs 31:26 NLT). Now that's respect! Ladies, you can't demolish him verbally and expect him to trust you, be passionate about you, and bare his soul to you. He might do those things for a little while, but if the tongue-lashings become more frequent … and more severe, he will either lash out physically or leave emotionally. The first option is never acceptable, but it's all too common.

One young couple had a history of breaking up to make up before they got married. Their fights were intense and abusive. I'm still not sure why any minister officiated a wedding for them. Maybe it was because they were so sweet and sentimental when they were in a good space. But when they were off, they were toxic.

I told you of the following incident earlier, but it bears repeating for its relevance to our present topic. One day I happened to call the husband while this toxic couple was in the middle of a heated argument. He picked up the phone but didn't say a word. All I could hear in the background was some lady I was sure hated him to the nth degree. Whoever she was, she had absolutely nothing kind to say about him. She said things to him that I'd never heard, even in my twenty years of ministry in collegiate and professional football locker rooms. Even now I can't believe the words that came out of that woman's mouth. That woman, I eventually discerned, was his wife. I knew then that it was unlikely the marriage could continue after that verbal beat-down.

I'd known the couple for some time. But I'd never known that those words were flying around in their marriage and in their home. I was saddened, shocked, and disappointed. It was clear to me that she had zero respect for him. He wasn't completely innocent, having failed her emotionally on many occasions. But I knew when I witnessed her verbal rage that no man would be able to take much more of that. If she couldn't respect him, he would at least have to respect himself enough to get out of the house. He's still out to this day. And sadly, they're dissolving their marriage. Rather than find a way to build him up with her words, she tore down her house, one astounding, tragic, cuss word at a time.

Ladies, I'm not suggesting that the story above is normal or usual. Perhaps it's hyperbolic, but the principle is the same. If you use your words to build up the men you care about rather than to tear them down, they will not be able to question your respect for them. Where they may fall short, your wise and kind words could be the difference that helps them get on track with God's purpose, plan, and vision for their lives. Your words have unimaginable power.

Respect Stands Down

Bright, strong, capable women are not hard to find. They're shining in corporate boardrooms, in academia, in politics, in medicine—just about anywhere you look. Many of the brightest and strongest women I know also have levels of responsibility and authority that are well-earned. That's a good thing and we should celebrate it.

That good thing can also present challenges, however, between women and the men they love and care about. That's especially true in marriages and relationships where women earn more than their men. It's also true in relationships where her work is a leadership role and his is not. Oddly enough, it's also true between big sisters and their younger brothers.

The question is, ladies, can you stand down and allow him to exercise authority in a situation that you are fully capable of handling, leading, or deciding? You see, men were made to carry the weight of ultimate responsibility, especially as fathers, husbands, and providers. Ultimate responsibility doesn't mean better or more capable. It simply means more accountable to God.

When God fashioned Adam, He gave him the "instruction manual" for life in the garden. It was Adam's responsibility to convey to Eve God's instructions to not eat from the tree in the middle of the garden. Those instructions were what God, ultimately held Adam responsible for. When Adam and Eve had both eaten from the forbidden tree, God didn't come looking for Eve. He came looking for Adam: "Where are you?" "Who told you that you were naked?" Both of them were hiding, and both of them were naked. But God came to Adam for a response that Eve could easily have given.

Men find respect like water finds the path of least resistance—moving away from its source and causing damage in the process. For a man, to live without respect is to live with disrespect. He can only live without respect for so long before he begins looking for someone or something who will offer it to him.

Ladies, a man is most a man when he's living and acting responsibly. He's his best when he's willing to take responsibility for the outcome of the things he's the leader and head of. He's responsible for his *garden*—i.e., his home, his family, his children, his finances. As Dr. Myles Munroe use to say, "When God presented Eve to Adam, she found him in the presence of God."[1] That means the man is responsible to remain in the presence of God, hearing His voice and carrying out His directives.

When a woman takes over a man's responsibilities, one of two things has happened. She has either grown frustrated with his lack of direction, leadership, and responsibility, or she has simply taken over because she doesn't understand how to let him lead. Too many women have had to assume responsibility and taken charge because of the negligence and absence of men. But others have simply taken over. They run the garden. They run it capably. That's because women are very capable leaders who are strong in their own right. God didn't make them weak; He made them *weaker*. That is, He made them weaker physically, but not weaker in every way. That simply means God made women with different strengths unlike those of the man.

Having been raised by a strong, single mother, I have some idea what a woman is capable of. But ladies, if you take over all the leadership from the man in your life, including sons you're raising, you undermine his ability to become the leader God designed him to be. He was designed to exercise leadership dominion for the wellbeing of his family, his children, his church, and his community. That doesn't mean he has permission from God to overpower and be authoritarian, terrorizing everyone in his wake with messy, masculine insecurity. It means he should be given room to fulfill his responsibilities.

When a woman oversteps her boundaries of responsibility, she makes the decisions unilaterally. In many cases, when questions arise that require a decision, she already knows the answer. But wisdom dictates that she stand down and give her husband or son or male subordinate the opportunity to speak to the matter. It's like my friend who knew that her daughter needed a car while away at college. Taking the bus at night and riding a bike had become a danger to the girl. My friend simply said to her husband, "Jessica called and said she needs a car. I told her she needs to speak with you because you're our leader. Just so you know, I'm already firm that we need to get it for her. But I don't want to undermine your leadership. So can you please get her the car she needs for her safety? I'll move out of the way so you can handle it." He did, and of course he looked like a hero to his daughter. But what wisdom his wife exercised by standing down. And what respect her husband felt from her.

Ladies, to stand down doesn't mean you surrender your wisdom and insights into matters. It doesn't mean you have to let your son or husband destroy a situation he's not proven to be wise enough to lead. What it does mean is that you invite his leadership. You invite his voice and perspective. You pray. You express your thoughts on the matter and look for a way to move toward the best solution. Of course, in the workplace where you have authority and the responsibility to produce, the end of the matter rests with you. Thank your guys for their input and make the final call. That's your space and that's your job. But where it's your man's responsibility, have the strength and the wisdom to stand down. Expressing respect for the man in your life always pays relational dividends.

He Will Get Respect One Way or Another

One final word about respecting him. Men find respect like water finds the path of least resistance—moving away from its source and causing damage in the process. For a man, to live without respect is to live with disrespect. He can only live with disrespect for so long before he begins looking for someone or something that will offer it to him. Like the famous comedian Rodney Dangerfield used to say, "I get no respect! I can't take it no more." Ladies, we men are so designed to receive respect, it's like the air we need to breathe.

I've known men, young and old, who are engaged in desperate searches for respect. It's not a pretty picture. When they're out of work or unable to generate income, then selling drugs, stealing, or scamming seems like great options. They put their names, families, and futures at risk just to make money and feel productive. I'm convinced most men who end up in jail are not by nature criminals. They were simply looking for respect.

I've seen good men leave beautiful wives with great careers. These were men with commitments to their faith in Christ and to their families. In almost every case, they wrestled for years with what to do about the disrespect they felt from their wives. They wanted their marriages. They wanted a legacy of family and faith. But the disrespect was too much; they settled for the legacy of faith and hoped they could maintain relationships with their children.

One close friend's adult daughter said to him as the marriage was deteriorating, "Dad, I don't know how you stay here. How do you take it? I won't blame you if you leave Mom. She's so disrespectful to you." Sure enough, after twenty-eight years of marriage, he couldn't take the name-calling and the attacks on his manhood. He wasn't perfect, but neither was he what she called him. And he is not the kind of guy who puts his hands on women. He's remarried now—to a woman who knows his shortcomings, supports his vision, and builds him up with her words. His ex-wife admitted to him at their son's wedding, "I really messed up. I didn't know how to respect you as a man." If only she had learned that earlier in their marriage, they might have been seated together at the wedding. He would have had no reason to look for the respect he desperately needed and wanted anywhere else.

Ladies, if there's going to be a healthy and fruitful relationship, there must be respect. If you have male friends or family members in your life who don't carry themselves in ways worthy of respect, remind them that there's more in them and more to them. Tell them you know it to be true because God created them. If you can't respect a man you are romantically attracted to, just back away from him. Make a clean break, because it's never going to work if you have no respect for him. (And certainly, if he doesn't demonstrate respect for you, let him go. You're too valuable to be stuck with someone who can't see the glory of God in you.) If you're married to him and you can't respect his person, then respect his assignment and the position God placed him in within the family. Pray for him to step into and up to the space God has ordained for him as a man. Remind him that you believe he can do this with God's help. God will bless your commitment to the principle of respect.

Chapter 3 Reflections:

1. Respect is something we feel. And we feel it deeply—down to the core of our being, down deep in our souls. We feel it when it's there. And believe me, we feel it when it's not there. We can absolutely feel when we are treated and regarded as someone worthy and weighty. Men feel respect.

2. God designed men in such a way that respect is core to our identity. Even as young boys, we grope for it among our peers. As we grow into our teen and adult years, we gain respect principally through our work and our ability to produce a living. How well we do our craft, face the challenges that come with it, and earn from it are a matter of respect for men.

3. Men find respect like water finds the path of least resistance—moving away from its source and causing damage in the process. For a man, to live without respect is to live with disrespect. He can only live without respect for so long before he begins looking for someone or something who will offer it to him.

4

Make Love To Him
Welcome Him To Worship
(*For Married Couples*)

One of the most common questions I receive when I speak at marriage retreats or men's conferences is this: "How often should my spouse and I have sex?" That question comes from men and from women. Either way, it's a loaded question. Usually, the person asking the question is under some degree of pressure to have sex more often, feeling sexually rejected, or trying to figure out why his or her spouse has such an active sex drive.

The tension that comes from a lack of sexual desire and intimacy is difficult for husbands and for wives. No one wants to feel undesirable or incapable of satisfying his or her spouse. Certainly, no wife or husband should be neglected when it comes to sexual intimacy. The damage that results from sexual neglect is emotionally and psychologically deflating. It can destroy a marriage if it's not resolved. Such neglect, whether intentional or unintentional, will take a serious and lasting toll on either marriage partner. Both become vulnerable to the hollow invitation of an affair, even when such a thought was once never an option. Sexual rejection can bring out the worst in the best people.

Responding to Rejection
We men respond to our needs for sexual intimacy in ways that are distinctive to our design. A woman who faces repeated sexual rejection from a spouse will absolutely find it painful. Her solution might be to shop and run up credit card bills, at first, attempting to relieve her frustrations, sadness, or anger. She might fill the longing for intimacy by turning to romance novels, binge scrolling on Facebook, or cuddling up with Netflix episodes hour after hour. She might find herself overeating or drinking too much alcohol to satisfy her hunger for her husband. She may even find herself angrily

and resentfully questioning her man's masculinity. At some point she may begin to ask, "What, am I not good enough?"

In most cases, a woman is looking for relational intimacy and physical connection. Women are designed by God with a need to feel loved and secure at the deepest levels. That's why Paul charges men in Ephesians 5:25, "Husbands, love your wives, just as Christ loved the church and gave himself up for her …." Sexual rejection robs wives of their deep need to feel loved. It's not that she doesn't need or desire the satisfaction and physical pleasure of intercourse. It's just that she receives something different from sexual play than a man does because her needs are different from his. So when sex is withheld from her, she defaults to other things that make her feel pleasure and connection. Yes, adultery with a person of the opposite sex or of the same sex can begin to feel like viable options in an attempt to fill the void of sexual connection in her life. But those extremes are usually not a wife's first consideration, because emotional and relational intimacy with the man she married is the more primary need for a woman within the act of physical sex. The exception to this norm can involve a woman's unresolved addiction to sex or a past of trying to meet her real need for love with sex. A wife's needs for relational and emotional connection *can* be experienced through physical touch and sexual pleasure, but they are not exclusive to them. She can also get those needs met through life-giving hugs from healthy, life-long relationships with her dearest girlfriends and loving family members.

> *Sexual acceptance, desire, and the ministry of sexual pleasure with your husband could be the loudest statement a wife can make to say, "I respect you."*

Women are built for love. That's why the saying, "Women are like ovens; men are like microwaves" makes sense. Often, a couple's love is expressed through conversation, thoughtful gifts, time together working on a home project, or snuggling up on the couch to watch a movie. It's true that some wives have a greater drive and desire for sexual pleasure than their husbands do and don't need all the foreplay. They can be ready to fly with a very short runway! As one woman wrote with frustration during a Q&A session at a recent marriage event where I was teaching, "My sex drive is greater than my husband's, and I get upset when he doesn't perform. There is an age difference, and I just need to know how to handle this." For a few women, sex may be the main event, but most women crave intimacy first.

Most consistently, sexual pleasure for women requires a longer runway of meaningful conversation, non-sexual touch, and gestures of care and affection. I usually hear some iteration of this statement: "I wish we could just lie down and cuddle and it not always turn into sex. I love it when we're just relaxing together in each other's arms. It makes me feel secure and loved. After I get to that place, I'm more than ready to have him sexually!" That's just not the case with men. I've never heard a man say he would prefer to cuddle first!

Men are very different from women when it comes to sexual rejection. Many of the married men I meet around the country who face constant sexual rejection feel beat down, lost, lonely, hopeless, and dejected. A lack of sexual interest on the part of many of their wives is draining their mental and emotional vitality. Often times, these are men of high caliber who work hard every day to provide for their families. They're conscientious and caring. In many cases they serve God faithfully in the marketplace and in the church. They are men doing their absolute best to be the finest husbands, fathers, and leaders they can be. But when their spouses are disinterested in pleasuring them sexually, these men often respond to the rejection with feelings of dejection. They may eventually go shopping for another sex partner, but never have I seen a man who's been repeatedly rejected sexually go shopping for another pair of shoes or sit around and indulge his appetite for Netflix. It's much more likely that he will turn his sexual appetite to pornography.

The pattern of a husband's emotional slide downward after repeated sexual rejection is typically dejection, resentment, depression, then anger. In other words, he goes from slumped shoulders and a sad countenance to bitter indignation that anyone could treat him like that. As the indignation runs its course, depression becomes a real issue, even if it's craftily masked and denied. The depression, if not arrested by effective soul care and counseling, will likely become anger or even rage, bursting outward unpredictably and in a variety of ways. And that's the stage where men become most dangerous to the other people and to themselves. The anger stage is where many rapists rape. According to The Center for Sex Offender Management, it's out of anger over feeling inadequate that some men connive to overpower and assert themselves against their targets of rape and sexual assault.[2]

Wives, I'm absolutely not saying your husband will resort to such an extreme expression of anger and rejection. I'm certainly not saying that a husband's addiction to pornography or deviant sexual behavior is your fault or your responsibility. Quite likely, his sexual addiction began long before you married. What I am saying, ladies, is that constant rejection of any sort can impact anyone on levels that are more significant than we might imagine. I know from personal experience that men's egos can be very fragile, and our self-esteem can suffer, contrary to popular belief. We are more human than perhaps we have let on or even understand ourselves.

After the scales of sexual rejection have been tipped in a husband's world, his perceptions become distorted. According to Dr. Sarah Hunter Murray, writing on the *Psychology Today* website, men's minds quickly lead them from "My wife doesn't want to have sex right now" to "My wife doesn't want me."[3] Our perceptions get hijacked in the most painful ways. At a minimum, we withdraw from any efforts to connect and dramatically reduce our advances. We withdraw because the possibility of being rejected yet another time is too real, too painful. It's not something we can stomach. At our worst, we become something far more dangerous than merely disappointed, indignant, or depressed.

A Dude's Design

It's important to understand, ladies, that sexual pleasure for a man is in some regards deeper than a need for physical pleasure. Sexual fulfillment helps husbands to experience aspects of his unique, God-given design when his wife welcomes his sexual advances and initiates sex with him. God designed men relationally and emotionally in such a way that respect and a healthy sense of power are at the core of his being. Healthy and right expressions of respect and power nourish our psyches, i.e., our inner selves. They affect how we see ourselves.

The degree to which any man feels strong and respected is the degree to which he presses into the challenges of life, including academic struggles, vocational direction, financial challenges, and even relationship losses. In the garden of Eden, God made Adam a person of power whose job was to shape and cultivate the vast garden landscape. Adam had a big job to do. While doing it, Adam had to resist the potential intrusion of Satan by obeying God's command not to eat from the tree of the knowledge of good and evil. God made it clear to Adam that by himself he was not adequate for the job when He said, "It is not good for the man to be alone. I will make a helper suitable for him" (Genesis 2:18). Adam needed the presence, the partnership, and the respect of Eve in his life.

God gave Adam the responsibility and authority to name each of the animals He had created and placed under Adam's care. Authority is one thing, and responsibility really needs no explanation except to say that God gave Adam plenty of it. Possessing authority and responsibility, Adam had two elements in a three-element equation. I'd like to suggest that Adam couldn't experience the third element—respect—until he was responsible to love, consider, lead, and cherish someone who was, like him, made in the image of God. I believe Eve brought the perfect expression of respect to Adam's life in the garden. Nothing else in creation could have provided it for Adam—not plants, not animals, not streams, not cars, not money, not even his work. I also believe Eve was the one who helped Adam understand the gift of authority (power) God had entrusted to him. Adam's deep, built-in need for respect would come principally from his relationship with Eve. *Alone* would not cut it. Adam could not experience the fullness of God's *good* without Eve in his life. Sin, of course, taints everything.

Let's go one step further. Anatomically, Adam was designed for penetration—an expression of strength and power. Eve, on the other hand, was designed, anatomically, for reception and conception. (Yes, we're talking genitalia, here.) Penetration is a powerful notion – though it was never intended by God to be a negative notion. Any substance such as dye that can penetrate another substance like leather is understood to have qualities of strength. When one army penetrates another's defenses, its power is made obvious. When one football team penetrates the defense of another football team, the strength of its offense is displayed. When one company begins to penetrate the market of a rival company, its viability becomes clear. In the same way, a man's welcome penetration of his wife is more than a matter of sexual pleasure for them. It's also an affirmation that she respects him, honors his strength, and appreciates the person he is. All of this assumes a healthy and reciprocal relationship of love and respect between them.

Because we're now treading in very sensitive waters, let me make some things clear. Just because God designed men to be inherently strong and powerful with a design for penetration does not give us men the right to abuse our strength. That is, in fact, what many men have done, as I discuss in my book *Cover Her.* Many men have abused their strength. We have expressed sexual desire selfishly, consuming women, destroying children, and even emasculating other men, sadly. Communities around the world are becoming more and more filled with sexual predators and victims of men's predatory practices. Sadly, the long list of accused predators include Catholic bishops, entertainment moguls like Harvey Weinstein, Kevin Spacey, and Bill Cosby, and Supreme Court justices Brett Kavanaugh and Clarence Thomas. Prison populations are replete with men whose only understanding and use of power is sexual assault. Twisted attempts to gain respect include stripping other inmates of dignity and masculinity. Women, however, have been the number-one target of men whose man-strength has become a weapon of sexual assault. Dark, demonic forces are wreaking havoc in pandemic fashion because many men use their power in disturbingly perverse ways.

I'd like to assume, for the sake of our conversation, however, that we're discussing men who do not pervert their man-strength—men who use their power for the good of others. Let's assume we're talking about men who are doing their best and trying to give their best to their wives and to others who depend on their leadership. Of course, nobody's perfect. Every man has made mistakes on the journey of life and marriage— some more significant and more damaging than others. We've all spoken insensitively to the wives we vowed to cherish. Many have struggled to make sure the bills were all paid at some point. More than a few men have had to admit to being unfaithful at some point in their marriage. Most of the men I know genuinely regret the seasons of folly and failure that brought temporary satisfaction to them but lasting pain to their wives. None of these failures should be carelessly dismissed without being intentionally addressed and taken up with a proven therapist who is biblically based. But they should not always be deemed perversions of power. Many of these men have demonstrated genuine repentance. They've admitted having sinned in quests to silence the pain of their own insecurities and feelings of inadequacy. Many have grown spiritually, emotionally, and relationally, and have regained respectability.

What I hear from many good men who do not abuse their power is devastating: "She won't make love to me, Rod. What is a man supposed to do? I feel so rejected. And now I feel trapped, because stepping outside of my marriage is the unthinkable sin to me. But she's only interested in sex three times a year!" One pastor friend confided to me that his wife withheld sex from him for over two years! The confusion, dejection, and the feelings of being mentally disoriented were almost unbearable for him. No wonder their twenty-year marriage didn't last. I can't imagine how he preached to and taught a congregation every week with any degree of clarity. The rejection nearly destroyed him and the church. Thankfully, he's remarried now and quite satisfied at home. And the church has recovered and continues to grow.

Benefits and Blessings

Sexual rejection can do a real number on even a good, God-fearing man. But the mutual ministry of sexual pleasure that the apostle Paul describes in 1 Corinthians 7:2-5 promotes wholeness in both spouses:

> But since sexual immorality is occurring, each man should have sexual relations with his own wife, and each woman with her own husband. The husband should fulfill his marital duty to his wife, and likewise the wife to her husband. The wife does not have authority over her own body but yields it to her husband. In the same way, the husband does not have authority over his own body but yields it to his wife. Do not deprive each other except perhaps by mutual consent and for a time, so that you may devote yourselves to prayer. Then come together again so that Satan will not tempt you because of your lack of self-control.

God's plan for sexual pleasure in marriage affirms a man's God-given design. It dignifies him. It bolsters his courage and builds up his confidence. It tells him that he's powerful in all the appropriate ways. It builds him up, reminding him that down on the inside he has something worthwhile to offer the world. It puts pep in his step. It relieves him amidst the stresses and pressures that come with his calling to cover his wife and children. It prepares him for the battles he must face head-on as the leader of his family—as protector, provider, praise leader, and presenter (see *Cover Her*). Dignifying a husband sexually is a safeguard to keep potential bouts with low self-esteem at bay. It's a powerful, protective barrier against temptations that can destroy a marriage and a family for generations. Sexual acceptance, desire, and the ministry of sexual pleasure with your husband could be the loudest statement a wife can make to say, "I respect you."

Ladies. Dear sisters. Señoras. If you married the man, please understand that sex comes with the covenant. God included it as a special, sacred, and necessary part of the marriage relationship. Hello!

Did you note in the Scripture passage above God's rationale for sexual intimacy in marriage? Sexual intimacy was intended as the answer and the antidote to keep believing spouses from getting trapped in destructive sexual immorality such as pornography, adultery, prostitution, incest, bestiality, homosexual behavior, and any other sexual behavior outside of the marriage covenant. Sex with your spouse is God's safeguard for both of you, to keep you from perverting something beautiful and turning it into something reprehensible to God. When that happens, painful and often irreversible consequences may ensue. God built you both with sexual needs and desires, but He placed boundaries around the gift of sexual expression so your sex lives would be an expression of worship that brings God glory.

Yes, even our sex lives are subject to the authority of God's word—not to our feelings, urges, and impulses. The best broad strokes for best practices and the best fulfillment are found in God's Word. "Put to death, therefore, whatever belongs to your earthly nature: sexual immorality, impurity, lust, evil desires and greed, which is idolatry. Because of these, the wrath of God is coming ... Whatever you do, work at it with all your heart, as working for the Lord, not for human masters, since you know that you will receive an inheritance from the Lord as a reward. It is the Lord

Christ you are serving" (Colossians 3:5-6, 23-24). In short, I'd say it this way: Fight for a healthy, God-honoring sex life with your spouse. If we leave it to chance, it'll never happen. But if we'll trust God and follow His lead, we'll be richly rewarded.

Resolving Tough Issues Realistically

To be sure, there are legitimate reasons for sexual disinterest. And quite possibly your husband may be the cause. Or perhaps it has nothing to do with him at all. Pain happens. Shame happens. Blame happens. Illness happens. Discomfort happens. I don't know what happened in your case, but I do know that the devil is happy to see you and your husband physically, emotionally, and sexually disconnected. He loves seeing you put asunder—with walls that have been slowly erected—the marriage God said no man should tear apart. And he loves to see your husband writhing in rejection, resentment, anger, and temptation. But now is the time to take your groove back from the enemy. It's time to begin building or rebuilding your fortress of marital love.

Men are very different from women when it comes to sexual rejection. Many of the married men I meet around the country who face constant sexual rejection feel beat down, lost, lonely, hopeless, and dejected. A lack of sexual interest on the part of many of their wives is draining their mental and emotional vitality.

It's not helpful to anyone to take an idealistic approach to the very sensitive, sometimes frustrating, and complex subject of marital sex. Good sex doesn't just happen. Problems are prevalent and people need solutions. For those reasons I'd like to offer you some help by answering a few legitimate questions I've received from women:

Q. How do I get my husband to understand when I'm sick or have a headache or am hurting internally and I physically cannot have sex?

A. Sometimes women suffer from pains and discomforts that men have no experience with—i.e., extreme menstrual cramping, fibroid tumors, painful ovulation, and vaginal dryness to name a few. Our bodies are different from one another's. Assuming you and your husband enjoy sexual intimacy regularly and seek to serve one another sexually, ask you husband if he ever has times when his body aches. Ask what sickness feels like to him. (This question came from the wife of an NFL athlete, which means he should've been well-acquainted with physical pain and how limiting it can be.)

When pain or sickness prevent you from having sex, let him know that you look forward to being with him—that you really want to, but you're in a lot of pain at the moment. Focus the conversation on how much you want to say yes, rather than on the fact that you are unable to. This can serve as a buffer against feelings of rejection that may surface in him. Ask him to try and understand, and reassure him that you are not trying to be selfish toward him. Let him know you really look forward to the connection with him.

Literally, pray that God will give him a spirit of understanding and that he will put himself in your shoes. Pray that God will help him focus more on how he can serve you rather than on how he can receive. If he's a selfish person, that will be difficult but not impossible. When he understands, it will clearly be an answer to prayer.

Finally, ask your husband if there's another way you can pleasure him sexually. You may be unable to have intercourse, but you may have enough energy to attend to his desires. I encourage couples to find other ways that they can mutually agree upon to meet the need for sexual pleasure in their marriage. This approach is often required during the physically awkward and uncomfortable latter months of a wife's pregnancy. You'll be amazed how creative you can become together. And I emphasize, *together*, not solo.

Q. "Just how frequent is frequent enough for sex in marriage?"

A. This question always concerns me for a number of reasons. Usually it represents deep disagreement about sexual intimacy. One spouse wants more sex, and the other partner finds it hardly necessary except occasionally. The question typically reveals that one partner or both have unhealthy perspectives about sex. One usually sees sex as distasteful and unwanted. The other may see it as something to obtain just for physical satisfaction, rather than as a gift from God intended to foster relational intimacy and bring glory to God.

To be sure, there is no right number of times daily, weekly, or monthly that a couple should enjoy sex. It may help to get numerically scientific as a way of finding agreement so both spouses are on the same page and have a plan to make sure they're making time for lovemaking. But really, frequency is more a matter of how spouses can serve one another. Everyone has days when sex is the last thing on his or her mind. Those are usually the days when it's heavy on our spouse's mind. Since sexual intimacy is an important ministry to one another in marriage, ask God to give you energy to give yourself selflessly to your spouse. You'll be amazed at how God can cause a shift in you when you purpose to honor your husband and God when you're just not in the mood.

If there are deeper unresolved issues such as abuse, adultery, dereliction of leadership duties, bills unpaid, depression, or some other matter beneath the surface, don't ignore them. Seek counseling. Try to start by talking with one another honestly if your communication is strong enough. Otherwise, call for support—a family pastor, a counselor, or another wise couple who has recovered from their own similar challenges. In the end, once a week or five times a week could be the magic number.

Q. "I recently discovered my husband has been having an affair. I don't trust him, and I don't want to be near him period—let alone, sexually. Not only am I concerned about getting a sexually transmitted disease, I hate what he has done to me."

A. Honestly, there may not be a worse pain than the pain of betrayal. This question or some form of it is all too common among wives whose husbands have cheated, betraying their trust. It's virtually unimaginable for a woman to want to be with her husband after discovering an affair, except when she believes she can prove herself to be the better woman by offering him superior sexual experiences. It never works, because sex is usually not the underlying issue.

Most men, unless they are sex addicts, do not commit adultery just because they're in search of yet another sexual encounter. In my experience, men who commit adultery do so in an attempt to address any number of emotional or personal issues in their lives. For some, another woman represents a life-long absence of motherly nurture. For other men, the affair represents an attempt to address deep feelings of inadequacy. In other cases, adultery represents a fix for feelings of rejection or experiences of disrespect. I've also known cases of adultery which were rooted in a man's attempts to overcome painful memories of childhood sexual abuse by older siblings, relatives, or neighbors—either male or female. This list of explanations is not exhaustive, neither does it excuse adultery. However, it may explain potentially unresolved issues that wives may not realize are hovering in the souls of their husbands.

So what should a wife do? There's no simple answer. But let me say this: Your marriage can survive an affair and be stronger than you ever imagined. As bad as an affair is, it can also be the best thing that happens to a marriage—a sort of wake-up call to both spouses. Romans 8:28 is still true: "And we know that in all things God works for the good of those who love him, who have been called according to his purpose." Rather than disengage from your marriage and give up on it, ask God for grace to get to the bottom of things. Let your husband know that you know and that you are open to fixing anything that you may have contributed to the condition of things. Be clear, however, that his choice to cheat is not your responsibility. Everyone is responsible for his or her actions.

Ask your husband if you can work together to find a marriage counselor that neither of you knows but who specializes in adultery. Ask him whether he plans to stop seeing his mistress(es) or whether he intends to continue. Ask him if he plans to leave the marriage and the family or whether he plans to fix what is clearly broken. Ask him if the two of you can be tested for STDs and be open about results. Let him know you hate what he's done, that you feel deeply wounded and rejected, but that you hope to be able to forgive him and to grow your marriage. I know all of this sounds abnormal, mechanical, and out of touch with the pain. But I find that there is a need for sobriety when adultery is discovered. Only truth can rebuild trust in marriage.

Ladies, this is where you'll need fortitude and a couple of good friends who can pray you through the storm. You'll be hit with a storm of fears, doubts, and ideas about what you should do to get even. Ask your friends to pray for you. Find one among them, or a mentor or spiritual leader, to whom you can fully unleash your feelings without judgment. You will be sad, hurt, and frightened, but try not to panic and try not to act desperate. On some level, it's just time to get down to the business of learning what the devil has been trying to do in your family and discovering God's bigger picture in it all. You can survive this!

I will not attempt to be a sex therapist, though my graduate degree is in counseling. My insights are not meant in any way to be a substitute for solid, biblical counseling, but rather broad strokes to infuse hope and to give you some direction. There are people such as Drs. Clifford and Joyce Penner who are established experts in sex therapy. I recommend that you arm yourself with material from their expansive and excellent body of work, which you can access at this website: https://fullerstudio.fuller.edu/contributor/cliff-joyce-penner/. I also believe you'll be greatly helped by the resources of Dr. Doug Weiss (www.drdougweiss.com). He's a tremendous guy with a brilliant handle on the issues of relational and sexual intimacy, and he relates these issues solidly to the Word.

Chapter 4 Reflections:

1. Men are very different from women when it comes to sexual rejection. Many of the married men I meet around the country who face constant sexual rejection feel beat down, lost, lonely, hopeless, and dejected. A lack of sexual interest on the part of many of their wives is draining their mental and emotional vitality.

2. A man's welcome penetration of his wife is more than a matter of sexual pleasure for them. It's also an affirmation that she respects him, honors his strength, and appreciates the person he is. All of this assumes a healthy and reciprocal relationship of love and respect between them.

3. Sexual acceptance, desire, and the ministry of sexual pleasure with your husband could be the loudest statement a wife can make to say, "I respect you."

4. Sexual intimacy was intended as the answer and the antidote to keep believing spouses from getting trapped in destructive sexual immorality such as pornography, adultery, prostitution, incest, bestiality, homosexual behavior, and any other sexual behavior outside of the marriage covenant.

5

Be His Companion
Let Him Know You're With Him

Many men live as loners. There are many possible reasons for this unfortunate phenomenon. Some of us feel misunderstood. So rather than continuing the oft-frustrating exercise of explaining ourselves, our pain, our fear, our wants, our dreams, and our desires, we settle for the "lone ranger" option on life.

Some of us are relationally challenged. We're great with tasks, projects, tools, and problems to solve. But if you press us to talk about our feelings, share our dreams, and share conversation over dinner every night, we are like fish out of water. It's not that we are not relational, it's just that doing is more important than dialogue for many men. Many of us were not raised to "be in touch with our feelings" and to be active listeners. The fathers many of us knew (if we knew them) were relationally aloof or simply low key. Dads who initiate conversation, express their feelings, and who say, "I love you" is a relatively new breakthrough, but still uncommon overall.

Don't hold it against us, ladies. We are relational. But we're not necessarily relational in the ways women are. (We still don't get how you and your girlfriend need to go to the ladies' room together when we're out at a restaurant with you!) Long phone conversations are a stretch even when we're courting you. Sorry. I know you feel duped after marriage begins and we stop talking as much. But from a man's task-oriented perspective, the main mission has been accomplished: We've won the prize! We usually relate on the basis of tasks, goals, and responsibilities—i.e., how well we've provided, what's on our plates to get done, how much farther the drive is, and what problems we can help you solve. Now that we've landed you, we have to change the mission to growing the intimacy so our actions will make sense to us.

We gravitate to the loner life, but being alone, according to God, "is not good" for men. We want your companionship even when we don't know how much we need it. But companionship for a man means something different than it does to a woman. It certainly means friendship, conversation, and time together. But often, for men it means joining us on our adventures and even taking an interest in our work. He needs to know you will go with him on play dates, i.e., while he's practicing his hobby. Will you take a long, quiet drive with him? (Talking is not necessarily required.) Can you enter into his unique world as an observer, learner, and celebrator? Maybe you're willing to learn to swing a golf club if that's what he does—or even ride in a golf cart for eighteen holes once in a while. Just taking an interest in his world is the key.

He needs you by his side on big days like office Christmas parties, award ceremonies, and long business trips. And he needs you in his ear whispering words of encouragement on days when he's fighting discouragement: "I'm praying for you. You're an amazing guy. You accomplished more than you're giving yourself credit for." To some men, companionship can be more important than romance. It provides the richness of friendship, closeness, shared experiences, relaxation, and recreation together, all of which adds meaningful support to a man's life.

There are five keys to companionship I believe every man needs and desires in his relationships with the ladies in his life. They are not exclusive to romantic or married relationships because the root idea of companionship is that of close friendship. Many men and women are companions with one another even when theirs is not a romantic relationship that involves sexual intimacy at all. And friendship companionship can certainly span male-to-female relationships, male-to-male relationships, or female-to-female relationships. But for the sake of our discussion, I will focus on the dynamics of marriage, dating, and engaged relationships between men and women because that's the focus of *Cover Him*. And my goal is to do all I can to let ladies in on the usually unspoken needs of the men they love.

Shared Experiences

George (not his real name) had been married for twenty-one years when he came into my office. Normally energetic and holding life by the tail, he was tired, tearful, and sad. He loved his wife but declared he just couldn't take it anymore. We had a unique relationship in that I was aware of his long life of infidelity. But so was his wife. Yet somehow, they remained together.

He was exhausted and frustrated, often trying to fill his need for companionship through relationships with other women. Home life was terribly boring, as he described it. And I've discovered that a man who's bored in life is far more dangerous than one who is always on a new adventure. "Susan doesn't like to do anything," he explained. "She won't go on trips with me. She won't go out with me on my motorcycle. She won't go out and dance with me. I love her because she's a great person. She's put up with my foolishness for years. But our marriage is boring and dull. I don't know what to do." Clearly, he was at an impasse. For years I'd encouraged him to be faithful to his wife and to go to counseling. He knew I could not and would not condone his adultery. Neither would I judge him. This was his breaking point.

That day a light came on in my mind. It wasn't just sex with other women that George was looking for. He loved the way women fussed over him, pushed back against his arguments, got dressed up to meet him, and went out to dance with him. I think his was an extreme case because he lost his mother when he was very young. He longed for the nurturing presence of a woman in his life—someone who paid attention to him and was with him on the journey, much like a good mother is in a son's early years of development.

What George was desperate for he couldn't get from his wife. He wanted someone who was interested in sharing the experiences of life with him—experiences that he enjoyed. Again, in no way and under no circumstances would I ever suggest that his adulterous betrayals of his wife were anything less than sinful. They were hurtful to his wife and harmful to his family relationships. But there was another betrayal that was being grossly overlooked. There was the emotional betrayal that often left George lonely, empty, bored, and wanting.

For some reason, his wife could not see the value and necessity of sharing in his experiences—what he called "living a little." She couldn't see that a part of her role in his life was to be a partner—a companion. I know his wife. Susan is a wonderful woman who is a conscientious mom and homemaker and a hard worker in her career. But it's not good for the man to be alone. Her very even and mellow personality was beautifully paired with his gregarious, outgoing temperament, for the most part. But he needed some spark from her occasionally—a willingness to do something other than the laundry and the cooking.

Perhaps she was never taught that she was made, in large part, to be his companion. Did Susan know that a perpetually immaculate home might not be what her husband needed most from her? Maybe a little less tidying and a little more dancing could change everything in their marriage.

He needs you by his side on big days like office Christmas parties, award ceremonies, and long business trips. And he needs you in his ear whispering words of encouragement on days when he's fighting discouragement: "I'm praying for you. You're an amazing guy. You accomplished more than you're giving yourself credit for."

Her parents had lived a humdrum existence in which her father cheated all the time. He was always gone, and Susan's mother, much like her, had been the dutiful wife, ever at home taking care of the laundry, the cooking, and the cleaning. Home was immaculate. But both marriages suffered deeply. I'm not sure if George and Susan have begun the practice of sharing experiences together. But I'm convinced that a little bit of stretching toward one another to share experiences, would change their marriage significantly.

Secret Places

My wife, Sheri, and I have secret places we go to that belong to no one but us. Well, that's not quite true, but I think you know what I mean. There are hotels, towns, back roads, specialty stores, and new destinations that we love taking in together. Some of them we share with our friends. But many of them we keep to ourselves. We treat the discoveries as "our little secrets." They represent new adventures and discoveries in our life together. Discovering new places is one of the things we love to do more than anything. It's one of the highlights of our twenty-eight years of marriage. I'll take the long way home—the scenic route—just so we can see a new place, a new development, a new store, or a new ice cream shop.

Having secret places that we've discovered together fuels my need for seeing more, learning more, and gaining new exposure. Sometimes I take roads that clearly, few people know about. It used to be that my wife would become nervous with fear and demand that I turn around when I took an unfamiliar backroad. I didn't understand. In fact, it made me furious because I felt that her fear was stifling my need for discovery.

One day we were traveling along the Eastern Shore of Maryland, not too many miles from our home. I saw a sign that said, "Childhood Home of Harriet Tubman, Conductor of The Underground Railroad." I was thrilled! I couldn't wait to find it. But at that time, the place was poorly marked. No problem. I was sure I'd find it. But the more we wandered the backroads of Cambridge, Maryland, the more lost we became. (Did I mention my four kids were in the back of our family Suburban?) My wife was becoming more and more uncomfortable, especially as I drove up to an interesting farm property. There we were greeted, none-too-warmly, by a group of older white men sitting under a Confederate flag.

Innocently but confidently I asked, "Can you tell me where the childhood home of Harriet Tubman is." Their one-word reply said it all. "No." My wife spared no words with me: "Why would you drive us up here? Back this truck up right now." That was probably not our greatest adventure, but it sure was memorable! We laugh about it every time we travel Highway 13 along the Eastern Shore of Maryland. We later discovered, by the way, that we were at the correct property. It was still owned at the time by the descendants of Harriet's slaveholders! It was a close call, but a wild memory—and one of our secret adventures.

I could name a hundred other places we've discovered together, including hole-in-the-wall restaurants and five-star hotels in other countries. Sure, lots of people know about them, but there's something about having discovered them together and keeping them as our little secrets that fuel closeness in our relationship.

Ladies, if a man wants to take you to a place that has special meaning to him—a childhood playground, a former place of employment from his youth, or his favorite college taco stand—he's cherishing your companionship. Please don't blow him off. Please don't say no. If it's not a dangerous place, go with him and make it yours together. If you discover a new place that sparks celebration, fun, and closeness in your relationship, make it "just ours." You don't have to buy it; just pretend you own it exclusively. Make it your little secret. If you run into friends there, just welcome them to your little secret spot. You'll never forget the adventure, and he'll never forget that you cherish with him a secret place.

Supported Celebrations

I'm one of those weird people who had to be taught the necessity of celebrations. I don't know what it is, but I prefer a quiet setting without too much fanfare. Sheri, on the other hand, celebrates her 4th of July birthday the entire month of July! That never made sense to me. So she has had to teach me not only how to celebrate milestones, birthdays, and accomplishments, but also how to enjoy being celebrated.

A few years ago, as I was wrapping up my graduate studies, my wife asked me who I wanted to come to the graduation ceremony. I wasn't even planning to attend the ceremony. I just figured I'd receive my diploma in the mail and go on with life and ministry. My wife was flabbergasted! "No sir," she said. "We are not doing that. Do you realize how proud of you your children and I are? You've started a church, earned two Super Bowl rings, been leading our family, and you found a way to complete your graduate studies. We're going to celebrate, and we're going to celebrate you."

I have to admit that it was one of the best days of my life. Not only did I walk and receive my diploma, the president of the college asked me to share some words about finishing strong. I was honored. My entire family was there to celebrate, including Sheri, our four college-aged young adults, my mom and stepdad, who has since gone to be with Jesus, and my two aunts. We call Aunt Ruth, Aunt Jean, and Mom the golden girls! We took pictures together, enjoyed a wonderful dinner out together, and laughed the day away together. Just thinking about that day makes me smile even as I write. What wonderful memories we created!

The celebration didn't stop there. Did I tell you my wife celebrates her birthday for an entire month? Well, when I got home, my house was filled with friends and leaders from my church. They greeted me with the loudest shout of surprise I'd ever heard in my life. They gave me kind and generous gifts, words of congratulations, and high-fives all the way around. It felt amazing ... after I got over the initial awkward feeling that people had set aside hours in their schedules to purchase thoughtful gifts, get to my home before me, wait for over an hour, and stay around to enjoy another meal.

That day of being celebrated did something wonderful for me. It brought a long and difficult journey of studies, papers, and classes to a perfect landing. It solidified in me the value of starting something big and finishing it well. It made me feel valued, acknowledged, and appreciated. I think it elevated my stock with my children: "Dad stuck with it and finished it, no matter how long it took. Our dad is not a quitter." It taught me that being celebrated matters and that it's healthy. More than all those things, I was reminded of how much my wife's support means in my life.

But remember ladies, none of this would have happened without her initiative and her being there. I know that some men don't need much reason to party. But there are others, like me, who need to be supported with meaningful celebration. They work hard. They give. They make sure that others are taken care of. They're always grinding. Celebrating them is a tremendous expression of companionship. I knew Sheri appreciated me, but that day of supportive celebration sealed it in me on another level. It reminded me that we are on the same team. As Al Jarreau sang, "We're in this love together!"

In 2 Samuel 6:16-23, Michal missed her moment to be a companion to her new husband, King David. She was the daughter of Saul, Israel's failed, first king. On the day that the ark of God was being brought into Jerusalem, representing the precious presence of God amongst His people, Michal insulted the king. Rather than celebrate alongside him as a companion, she watched from a window of the palace. She was disgusted that King David would dance to the point of coming out of his clothes—and that in front of a host of slave girls.

This was a day of victory and celebration for King David. After years of being hunted by Saul, not only was he establishing his place as the leader, but he was establishing God's place as number one in the nation. Rather than support the king in his celebration, she met him at the door with insulting words that dishonored and belittled him. David's reply: "I will celebrate before the LORD. I will become even more undignified than this."

Michal's unwillingness to support her husband's biggest day on the job to that point changed their relationship completely. What looked like a hopeful union became a lifeless, divided marriage. Verse 23 says it all: "And Michal daughter of Saul had no children to the day of her death." What is implied is that David refused to draw near to her, intimately, sexually. It seems David developed, rather quickly, a severe disdain for Michal. He was so hurt that he put her away and never touched her. He withdrew from her himself and his affection. How different their relationship could have been had she simply celebrated the king and his accomplishments.

Ladies, if you want to know how to bring out the best in the men you love, be a companion who supports him in celebration. Celebrate his big accomplishments and even his little ones. Acknowledge his progress and his impact. Take note of his achievements and lead the procession in celebration. He will never forget the companionship it displayed and the way it made him feel.

Silly Playdates

We bought a kayak last summer. We got it so we could row together, share some new adventures, and make some discoveries in one of our secret places near the beach where we fell in love. Let's be clear here. Neither of us had ever kayaked before, but Declan and Simonette had been doing it for years. Declan is our brother-in-law; Simonette is Sheri's sister. They made it look like so much fun in their Facebook videos … except for the time recently when the US Coast Guard had to rescue them!

But back to our kayak. We did all the research, found a good one on Craig's List, talked the seller into delivering it, purchased life jackets and water shoes, and off to the water we went. The only place we could get into the water without having to buy a cartop carrier is from a dock on a small harbor. "No problem. We'll figure it out," we said. So we packed lunch, sunscreen, water, sunglasses, and headed to the water. I did almost forget the oars. But we got everything we needed into the storage compartments just fine.

We had no idea that lifting a kayak off the storage rack and lowering it to the dock required such skill and athleticism. After we managed to get it lowered onto the water platform, we looked at each other. "Oh, we have to put it in the water." We climbed down to the platform from the dock, put the kayak in the water, and asked, "Now who's going in first?" We both can swim, but it wouldn't be a good look for us to capsize before we even get to push off on our maiden voyage! The entire endeavor was a total scream. From the purchase to trying to figure out the first push-off, we nearly laughed our heads off.

Somehow, we finally managed to get both ourselves off the platform, into the kayak, and rowing in the harbor. It was amazing! Our first cruise on "Baby Blue" (we named the kayak) took us places on the harbor where we'd never been. It gave us a different perspective, seeing the harbor and the inlet from the water. We even came up with a silly saying: "The couple that rows together grows together."

Sheri has been helping me not to take myself, my life, and my work too seriously. She's been teaching me how to have more fun and enjoy the journey. Her companionship gives me the freedom to be and to look silly sometimes. I get to step out of my leadership shoes, away from the stresses of ministry, and into my relaxation shoes. Silly playdates with her get me away from agendas and responsibilities. They help us to forge a deeper friendship—just as they do for kids.

Some of us men are relationally-challenged. We're great with tasks, projects, tools, and problems to solve. But if you press us to talk about our feelings, share our dreams, and share conversation over dinner every night, we are like fish out of water.

You might not know it, but silly is biblical! And it's a good barometer of your friendship with the man in your life. Are you able to be silly together? There's a beautiful description of the patriarch Isaac, in his younger days, with his wife, Rebecca. Having encountered a famine, Genesis 26 describes how they went to Abimelek, king of the Philistines in Gerar. While there, Isaac lied to the men about his wife, saying she was his sister. That was his strategy for saving his life in the event the men decided to kill him and take beautiful Rebecca for themselves. But a silly playdate gave away the truth of their relationship. Genesis 26:8-9 (NIV) says, "When Isaac had been there a long time, Abimelek king of the Philistines looked down from a window and saw Isaac *caressing* his wife Rebekah. So Abimelek summoned Isaac and said, 'She is really your wife! Why did you say, "She is my sister"?' Isaac answered him, 'Because I thought I might lose my life on account of her'" (italics mine).

The word *caressing* in verse 8 literally means *to laugh or play in merriment*! Isaac and Rebecca were having a moment of laughter, playing together. What strikes me is that they were able to play while in the middle of a famine and while his life was potentially in jeopardy. Even in a stressful situation, their companionship remained strong. It was so strong that it not only exposed the truth of their relationship to Abimelek the king, it actually saved their lives! The king gave orders that, "Anyone who harms this man or his wife shall surely be put to death" (Genesis 26:11 NIV).

That's just like God, isn't it? Only He could save our lives through faithful companionship. Who knows, ladies, you could be saving your man's life when you enjoy silly playtime together. Sometimes we need it and don't know it. Sometimes the grind takes us under, and we can't see beyond it. Before we know it, the stress that comes from constant work and wear begins to take its toll—high blood pressure, high cholesterol, weight gain, unusual pains, and difficult-to-diagnose symptoms. A real companion knows the value of time to be silly.

Sacred Confidant

Sisters, can your man tell you his secrets? I mean his innermost thoughts, desires, feelings, fears, and dreams? Okay, maybe he can tell you, but can he trust you to keep them a secret? Can you "keep his mail," so to speak? Psalms 44:21 says, "[God] knows the secrets of the heart." Proverbs 11:13, however, says, "A talebearer reveals secrets. But he who is of a faithful spirit conceals a matter." Companion means confidant.

You probably know already that we men do not share our secrets, readily. I've known men who lost their jobs in January and their wives didn't find out until August. I've seen men hold the difficult news of illness without telling anyone. They literally died with their secret. In no way am I suggesting that's healthy. I'm just making the point that men don't share secrets easily. But it's not just our secret disappointments or failures that we hold close to the breast. The same goes for our secret feelings, our secret dreams, our secret aspirations, and the secrets to our successes. Often times we even keep the good stuff to ourselves … except when we have a trusted companion.

Ladies, for a man to bare his secrets to you is put a rare stamp of approval upon you that deems you his trusted friend. Doing that is like giving you the most sacred part of his life. Our secrets play a big part in making us who we are—the good, the bad, and the ugly. In fact, I think it's safe to say we are our secrets. Our secrets drive us or stop us on the road of life. They talk to us, sometimes all day long. They inform our decisions and dictate our motivations. A man cannot be separated from his secrets. So if he shares them with you, he has just given you himself in the most intimate of ways.

So here's my admonition to you, sisters. Please do not take this trust lightly. Please do not tell his secrets without his permission (except in the case that he plans to harm himself or someone else). And please, do not pull a Delilah on a man. You remember Delilah? She was Samson's girlfriend from Sorek. She wanted to know the secret of Samson's strength—i.e., what made him seem invincible. The unfortunate truth of the Samson and Delilah saga in Judges 16 is that she was shopping for his secret so she could benefit financially.

Delilah was hired to ply him for his innermost insights. Samson was physically strong, but by the time he hooked up with Delilah he was spiritually weak. He had abused his strength and disobeyed God by touching the honey! No, not the kind of honey you're thinking of, but he had taken the honey that bees had made using the carcass of a dead lion as their hive. You see, Samson was under a strict, lifetime Nazirite vow, which included an injunction against ever touching a dead body. He lacked discernment; he didn't realize Delilah wasn't for him; she was for herself and for those who paid her to help them bring down the strong man. Delilah wore him down, day after day harassing him for his secrets. And Samson finally gave in.

The secret of Samson's strength, which he eventually revealed, was not his hair. More accurately, it was his head. Judges 16:16-17 says,

> And it came to pass, when she pestered him daily with her words
> and pressed him, so that his soul was vexed to death, that he told

her all his heart, and said to her, *"No razor has ever come upon my head, for I have been a Nazirite to God from my mother's womb.* If I am shaven, then my strength will leave me, and I shall become weak, and be like any other man." (italics mine)

Samson's strength came from the fact that he was under the headship of God almighty. His hair merely symbolized, physically, the spiritual truth. He was under a Nazirite vow that required him to abstain from drinking alcoholic beverages, touching dead carcasses, and cutting his hair. Samson played around with his vow, which was his secret. He ate honey out of a dead lion and let Delilah play in his hair. That's too close for comfort. And he told her his secret, thinking he could protect himself from any attacks she might bring against him.

What he should have known but couldn't discern was that she would be the one to bring about his downfall. She wanted his secret so she could reveal it to his haters, who would in turn use it against him. Okay, here's the point ladies: Don't be a Delilah. Don't tell people his secrets that he hasn't given you permission to tell. Don't expose his weakness or his strength to people who can't handle either and who don't need to know. Who knows who will turn on him years after you have shared his secret.

If companionship is your goal, then sacred confidentiality is a must. Don't tell your girlfriends what he fears most. Don't tell your brothers what he's dreaming of. His secrets are his—even after he has shared them with you. Don't have strangers looking at him with contempt or with vicious fangs waiting to pounce on him at the right moment of weakness. If you're his companion, keep his secrets, treating them like sacred treasures that belong to him alone. A failure to do so will create and establish doubt that could potentially destroy your relationship. Once it's clear that you were unable to keep a confidence, he may never be able to see you in the same way. If you will keep his secret, it will knit your hearts together and deepen his trust in your relationship. It will make clear that you are with him as a true companion.

Chapter 5 Reflections:

1. Some of us men are relationally-challenged. We're great with tasks, projects, tools, and problems to solve. But if you press us to talk about our feelings, share our dreams, and share conversation over dinner every night, we are like fish out of water.

2. He needs you by his side on big days like office Christmas parties, award ceremonies, and long business trips. And he needs you in his ear whispering words of encouragement on days when he's fighting discouragement: "I'm praying for you. You're an amazing guy. You accomplished more than you're giving yourself credit for."

3. Did Susan know that a perpetually immaculate home might not be what her husband needed most from her? Maybe a little less tidying and a little more dancing could change everything in their marriage.

4. If companionship is your goal, then sacred confidentiality is a must. Don't tell your girlfriends what he fears most. Don't tell your brothers what he's dreaming of. His secrets are his—even after he has shared them with you.

6

Give Him Your Ear:
Let Him Know You're Listening

One of the most important tools for life that God has given men and women is our voice. It is the tool we use to reveal our thoughts, our feelings, and our ideas. It is also what we use to express our desires and wishes. Our voices are what we use to create order, establish our boundaries, and exercise our authority. A man's voice in particular is what God has given him to lead his family and to accomplish his work. Having been created in the image of God, men and women are both designed to speak life into others and chaos into order. Everyone needs to be heard, and men are no exception to the rule.

As a father of three daughters and one son, dinners around the table always bring rich, oftentimes loud and sometimes dramatic conversation. As a family we love it because we always feel closer after a meal together filled with valuable dialogue. But there's always a challenge we have to face with four women sharing conversation with two men. My wife and our three daughters can simply out-talk Jeremy and me. Sometimes we can hardly finish one thought without their next thoughts peppering the atmosphere. We all have very strong viewpoints, and whenever we're all together, the talk is rich and lively.

I used to think my girls were just rude and needed some home training. But my wife helped me understand that in their all-girls school environment, talking across each other's ideas and finishing each other's thoughts was usual fare in an estrogen-saturated atmosphere. It's the way they process while learning and during conversation. I was relieved to learn that. I thought one of their parents forgot to give them some home training. But their conversational style was still a challenge for their super-introverted brother. I noticed that the more they bantered back and forth and in and out of the conversation, the less interested he became in sharing. For all of us, that was unfortunate, because Jeremy has one of the brightest minds we know. When he speaks, it's always worth listening because he never says anything flippantly, without thought or justification.

We had to figure out what to do so everyone could contribute to the discussions. So what do we do? I just remind my daughters, even to this day, "Please let me finish my statement." Or, "Please let your brother complete his thought." They don't mean any harm. It's just a difference between the women and the guys—at least in our family and likely in yours too. Most research suggests that women speak about 250 words per minute compared to a man's 125 words in the same time span. In the course of a day a woman may speak 25,000 words compared to a man's 12,000 words. Once the ladies are aware, we're all good to continue the conversation. And we're always glad we had it.

Ladies, most of the men you know need more time to process their thoughts before they can respond in conversation. It's a real thing. Our brains are wired differently. We communicate to solve problems or to relay critical information that will help toward the solution. We're usually trying to cut to the chase and get to the bottom line. We're asking ourselves, "What's the solution?" Most women, however, communicate to get things out in the open and off their chests. Neither approach is better—just different. So when a guy disconnects from the conversation, it's because he's either a little frustrated or experiencing word exhaustion because he can't get a word in edgewise. He's not being heard.

> *If you want to nurture your relationship with a man, you'll have to give him your ears more than your words.*

For that reason, when a man's voice is persistently, consistently unheard, unconsidered, or flat-out ignored, negative things can begin to happen, especially in the context of a relationship with the lady in his life. I've seen men who find it difficult to be heard at home become attracted to the lady at work who always seems to be interested in his ideas. Isn't it interesting that the Delilah who brought down the strong man, Samson, "lulled him to sleep on her knees" (Judges 16:19). Apparently, the harlot took an attractive interest in the mystique of his life. Samson's wife had been burned to death, and I surmise that he became a lonely man with no one to hear his innermost thoughts. Samson was strong on one hand, but weak and lonely on the other.

When talking at home or to the one who matters most to him yields no fruit, a man will literally shut down and turn off. He will limit his conversation to only what's necessary, or less than that. So ladies, realize that we're built with different capacities for communication. If you want to nurture your relationship with a man, you'll have to give him your ears more than your words. Below are some practical tips for letting a man know you're attentively listening to him.

Appreciate His Ideas

Ideas come in many sizes, shapes, colors, lifespans, and degrees of worth. Great ideas have no value until they have been expressed and acted upon. That's why an idea that's trapped inside a man's brain will never yield him an income stream. And an idea that never receives a hearing when it's expressed will not have the blessing and the benefit of helpful feedback or forward movement. Your listening adds value to his ideas, even if they're not quite fully developed and ready for prime time.

As you know, it takes a lot for many men to finally spit out what they've been contemplating in their minds. Sometimes it may be something we've been musing about for years. It's risky to "put it out there," knowing people might think it's a ridiculous, unrealistic, Martian of an idea. One of the fastest ways to get a man to stop sharing his thoughts with you is to tell him how ridiculous his thoughts are. They might be … but so what? Let him get them out. Your relationship with him is more important than you being right. It's just an idea.

If he knows you appreciate his mind and the articulation of his thoughts, he can handle it when you tell him, "That's a great idea. It'll be a stretch, but who knows what could happen with a strong plan." Or maybe you really have to say, "Honey, you come up with some amazing ideas. I love hearing how you think. This one, though, seems a little out there. But I love your brain. Don't stop sharing." Remember, you're covering him. And part of what it means to cover him is to appreciate him enough to give your thoughtful, engaging attention to his ideas.

Acknowledge His Angle

Okay, I know that you and the man you love never have disagreements and "intense fellowships" with higher-level decibel exchanges. But Sheri and I do. After all she's a Trinidadian, and in her culture, theatrics and drama are a way in life at home. I noticed it in her ninety-eight-year-old grandfather before he went home to be with Jesus. As we like to say, "Norms was full of drama." He, like my wife and her parents and siblings, was a passionate person.

But I'm fiery myself. I like a good argument. I love the exercise of debate. It's fine if I win, but that's not the point for me. The point for me is for us to have the discussion and together gain an understanding of one another. In my mind, if we can do that, we can grow in our relationship. I'm a passionate leader and I'm argumentative by nature. That means I'll do whatever it takes and take as long as necessary to get you to grasp my rationale.

As you'd imagine, this makes for some very intense conversations between Sheri and me. Okay, let's call them what they are … arguments. But we do have ground rules when we argue: Never attack the other person, and never disrespect the other person. We laid those ground rules in our first few weeks of marriage. We didn't do it because we were so smart. We made the rules because we realized we needed them. After all, we got married with the full intention of staying married for the rest of our lives. It's hard to enjoy your marriage or any other relationship when you know the other person will readily attack, demean, or disrespect you.

As with any other debate, i.e., with co-workers, friends, or family, it's crucial that we make a legitimate effort to see things from the other person's point of view. It's important that we be mature enough to validate the other's perspective, recognizing that our own perspective is not the only one in the world. Authors Mark Goulston, M.D. and John Ullmen, Ph.D. wrote in their book *Persuade Without Pushing and Gain Without Giving In* that there are three ways to engage people where they are in an effort to succeed together. That's what acknowledging one another's angles is all about—succeeding together in the relationship.

Goulston and Ullmen recommend the following: (1) Show that you get "it" by demonstrating Situational Awareness. In other words, what factors are impacting the conversation? Hunger? Illness? Worry? Exhaustion? Most arguments and disagreements don't happen in a vacuum. They happen in the context of life's ups and downs and a day's challenges. (2) Show that you get "them." That means show some Personal Awareness. Who is this person? What matters to him? What has he always valued? What's important to him? (3) Show that you get the other person's path to progress. Solution Awareness demonstrates your keen sense of how he thinks about solving problems. Does he normally need a few days to contemplate? Does he normally talk to a mentor? Does he make decisions quickly or slowly? What is his normal risk tolerance?[4]

Ladies, when you're in a disagreement with the man you love, it's unproductive for both of you to be so focused on winning the battle that you lose the war. You could be right and destroy a valuable relationship. Often when a man is in a heated exchange with the lady he loves, all he really wants to know is whether "she gets me." The issue of the discussion is secondary to the value you place on Personal Awareness. If you get him, he'll give you the argument in many cases because once he feels heard and understood, then he can hear that he's wrong. I'll say more about "getting" him in a later chapter because it's crucial to having a growing and productive relationship with your man. But for now, just know that one of the best ways to grasp his perspective is to ask him insightful questions.

Ask Him Insightful Questions

Let's start by getting one thing straight. Most men don't appreciate being asked a lot of questions, especially if they have no relation to his life, his work, his family, his objectives, or his interests. Okay, now that we got that out of the way, the rest will be a breeze. When I say to ask him insightful questions, the operative word is *insightful*. In. Sight. Full. Insightful implies looking into and seeing something or someone fully.

I think most people will tolerate a few rather abstract or irrelevant questions. Some men will, for sure. But if you want to let your man know that you're tuning into his life—that you're interested in what interests him—then your questions will reflect such thoughtfulness and make a huge difference in your journey together. They should help you gain insights into who he is and what matters to him. Your arsenal of questions should not end with, "What did you eat today?" or "Who won the game?" There's nothing wrong with those questions, but they don't give you insight into him. And likely they won't deepen your connection with him.

A man knows you're interested in him and giving him your ear when you ask questions that tap his deepest well of interests and needs. If he's a musician, ask him to explain the difference between the upright piano and a baby grand, for example. If he's a truck driver, ask him what helps him stay motivated to take care of the family when he's on the road by himself on long trips. Ask him what he thinks about when the weather gets bad. Is he a surgeon? Ask him how he went about preparing for the day's caseload. Did anything worry him about the day's procedures or outcomes? Ask how you can pray for his practice and his patients. These days, medicine requires great business acumen to succeed. If your man is into sports, go beyond "Who's your favorite player?" and add, "What do you admire about your top ten players and what about them do you like to emulate on your journey as a man?"

I'm a guy, and I've spent the majority of my ministry career talking with, counseling, and coaching men. We're fine with questions as long as they intersect with our lives and our priorities. When a woman asks those kinds of questions, good men feel considered, honored, and valued. For you to ask insightful questions says that you gave thought to the person he is, what matters to him, and what's a part of his life at the time. By the way, you don't have to ask ten questions in a day. That's way too many for most guys. But when my wife asks me one or two insightful questions, they usually spark a rich and engaging conversation. My defenses don't go up. My attention is hers, and I can tell she's tuned in to me and ready to listen to my sometimes-silly rants and my inner contemplations. I find myself more drawn to her because of her efforts to enter my unique, male world.

Honestly ladies, that's what many men complain about more than you might imagine. They feel unattended to and unnoticed apart from paying the bills and keeping the house and the cars maintained. Few of us have anyone who is tuned in to our needs and the ways we foster connection as men. "Unnoticed" is often code for *lonely.* And male loneliness is growing rapidly, becoming a common phenomenon for men around the globe. (For more on the male loneliness phenomenon, see *The Truth About Male*

Loneliness at https://www.menshealth.com/uk/mental-strength/a759609/the-truth-about-male-loneliness/).

Many guys wonder whether they matter apart from what they are expected to bring to the table financially and materially. As one frustrated husband wrote to me, "I feel that my wife has no interest in my career. She only cares about the money I bring in. Am I wrong for feeling used?" This guy is not only struggling, feeling unappreciated for his efforts to provide. He is lonely. And a lonely man is a dangerous man—both to himself and to those who need him most. A lonely man is ripe for costly temptation and poor decision-making. The tempter uses loneliness to lead men and women to some of our worst mistakes.

So ladies, when you ask your guy questions, try to make them count. It may take a while to get the hang of it, but he will appreciate your earnest efforts. It lets him know you're curious to know him better because he matters to you. Your listening to his answers will speak volumes to him and will fuel intimacy between the two of you.

Avail Yourself Fully

Finally, the list of things jockeying for our attention in our fast-paced, tech-filled world is amazing. Smartphones, smart TVs, tablets, Facebook, Twitter, and Instagram are at the top of that list. According to www.socialmediatoday.com, the average person spends two hours per day on social media. That adds up to a whopping five years and four months over a lifetime. According to Nielsen, the market-watch group, "American adults spend more than eleven hours per day watching, reading, listening to or simply interacting with media …."[5] Another recent statistic I read says that married couples in the U.S. spend about twelve minutes per day talking to one another—and not necessarily in meaningful conversation.[6] There's no question about it: we are focused on something. But it's not people. I think it's safe to say we are distracted.

The ease with which we can be distracted makes it difficult for any of us to be "all there" with anyone. It's taking a toll on friendships, marriages, and relationships of all sorts. It's nearly impossible to be in any social or public setting and not have our heads bent toward our devices, scrolling through social media posts, checking emails, or reading our news feeds.

It's pretty remarkable how much easier it is to be tethered to devices for information than it is for us to stop and relate face-to-face with real, live humans.

I know. I'm a little old school on this. I use social media out of necessity, not out of commitment. Facebook all but lost me with their information debacle. And I know a lot of men who wish their wives and significant others would just lose their devices and social media accounts altogether. (There are a lot of wives who need their husbands to do the same for a host of reasons, including addictions to pornography.) It's not likely to happen, but I certainly understand the sentiment. But devices and social media aren't the real culprits; people are. We are losing our ability to socialize deeply and to be fully engaged with people wherever we are. It's affecting relationships between men and women. And both sexes are guilty—including me at times.

I have some simple solutions, ladies, for how you can be fully available, with open ears for the man you love, without having to throw your devices into the neighborhood pool. Try turning off your phone, whenever you can, when you're spending time together. You may feel as if you're going to die. You won't. Give the babysitter the number to the restaurant; she can use that number while you're dining. Agree to times when you both will check your phones—maybe every twenty or thirty minutes, but not every two or three minutes. There are times when I intentionally leave my device in the car so I won't be tempted to check it when I'm with Sheri. When we go for walks, for example, we leave our phones in the car. And it makes a huge difference in our ability to enjoy the time together.

Of course, there are those times when we're riding in the car together and my wife spontaneously scrolls her Facebook or Instagram accounts. (I'm usually the driver.) It used to spark a fight in the car: "Can you just be here with me without having to cruise your Facebook page or text your girlfriends?" I'd bark. I used to think I was out to lunch in doing this until I discovered that many of my buddies were having the same conversation with their spouses. The solution in our marriage goes like this: (1) "Could you please not disappear silently, without a heads up, into your phone without acknowledging that I'm here?" (2) "If you must look at your phone while we're together, can you just give me a courtesy alert? That way I feel my presence has been acknowledged." And (3) "How about including me in on the good news? When you come across something funny or interesting, share it with me so I'm included." We find these solutions keep us connected while social media is in our space, rather than letting it foster resentment and divide us.

I used to feel that I was being a whiny wimp when I wanted my wife's attention. And I thought I'd be sacrificing my masculinity if I verbalized my desire for her attention. But quite the opposite has happened. My wife appreciates the gentle clarity and my willingness to be emotionally vulnerable. I have learned to express to my wife when I need her fully devoted attention. I especially enjoy it when we're together. Sometimes we're together but need to give our attention to a separate matter. That's life. But we also realize that life is short. Before we know it, we'll be older and someday in heaven. Most other things, like Facebook posts, can wait. Wouldn't it be a shame to have to wish we could get five years back that we gave to things that distracted us such as devices and social media.

Chapter 6 Reflections:
1. Ladies, most of the men you know need more time to process their thoughts before they can respond in conversation. It's a real thing. Our brains are wired differently. We communicate to solve problems or to relay critical information that will help toward the solution. We're usually trying to cut to the chase and get to the bottom line.

2. If you want to nurture your relationship with a man, you'll have to give him your ears more than your words.

3. One of the fastest ways to get a man to stop sharing his thoughts with you is to tell him how ridiculous his thoughts are. They might be … but so what? Let him get it out. Your relationship with him is more important than you being right.

4. Many guys wonder whether they matter apart from what they are expected to bring to the table financially and materially. As one

frustrated husband wrote to me, "I feel that my wife has no interest in my career. She only cares about the money I bring in. Am I wrong for feeling used?"

7

Feed Him:
Food Still Means Something To A Man

Because this subject is particularly sensitive, let's begin with some interesting Bible facts. The preparation and serving of meals occupy a lot of real estate in Scripture. The theme appears early in Genesis and becomes the devil's tool of temptation (Genesis 2:8-17; 3:1-7). In Genesis 15 and 18 the LORD appears to the patriarch Abram, who responded in awe by preparing time-consuming meals for Him—a show of humble gratitude and hospitality. In Psalm 23, food was a symbol of God's favor for King David as He was declared the God who "prepares a table for us in the presence of our enemies." A married woman in Shunem not only built a guest room onto her house for the prophet Elijah, she also fed him every time he traveled through town. She and her husband honored the man of God and demonstrated their care for his basic needs, which included food (2 Kings 4:8-10). In the Gospels, the miraculous power and generosity of Jesus are proved by the feeding of the 5000 and the 4000 (Matthew 14:21; 15:38). Food is everywhere in the Bible!

Food was important to our human experience then, and it's important now. The question that we must ask and answer is, "Why do men tend to want women to cook for them?" I bet you've been wondering the same thing, especially if you're not particularly fond of cooking. And if you're not interested in cooking for a man, there's no judgement. My assignment in this chapter is simply to help ladies understand *why* doing so with love and care means a great deal to most men.

If the man you love has not expressed a desire for your culinary care in his life, then you're free to move on to another chapter of in this book. But only do so after a candid conversation. Ask him, "Would you feel more cared for if I took time to cook for you or if I worked at becoming a better cook?" Would it matter to him? Ask him to be honest. But be ready for his honest answer. He may have been suppressing his real feelings on the matter, not wanting to hurt your feelings or not wanting to seem needy. It's possible he may have been forced to choose between having you without meals or not having you at all. Of course, he made the wiser choice if he married you (smile). But it's quite possible that he didn't choose honestly. That's for you and him to discuss. And I really hope you will.

Food is not just physical; it is also theological. It must have theological meaning because God provided it for Adam in the garden—even before He put Adam in the garden. Adam was created to require food, and the Source for his supply of food was clearly God. Adam could not separate his food supply from his Maker. The supply was abundant, but it was not without boundaries.

I can't tell you exactly why this is so, but God has allowed the satisfaction from food warmly, lovingly, thoughtfully, and tastefully presented by a woman to a man, to speak to a deep need in a man's life.

Food is relational in its nature as well. The forbidden tree that Adam and Eve bit from negatively affected their relationship with God and with each other. Remember, Eve ate first because she was deceived by the serpent. But she shared some with Adam and he also ate it, according to Genesis 3:6. Notice how the devil used food to drive a wedge between God and man and between man and woman. Food was at the center of the fall. It was at the center of the divide between the man, Adam, and his wife, Eve. Adam and Eve would spend the rest of their lives recovering from bitterness and blaming and from the regret of a fractured relationship—all because of food.

Their lives together could have been very different had Eve eaten from and offered Adam something from a tree that God had approved. Imagine how satisfied both of them would be. Imagine how different their relationship would have been. Imagine how different the world might be without sin and its consequences. Eve could have been building Adam up as his "helper suitable" rather than aiding his demise. Adam could still be celebrating Eve as "bone of my bones and flesh of my flesh" (Genesis 2:23) rather than complaining to God, "The woman you put here with me—she gave me some fruit from the tree, and I ate it" (Genesis 3:12).

I know it seems extreme, but a brief perusal of Genesis 1–3 makes this point about the importance of food clear. Isn't it interesting that man's final gathering with God in Revelation 19:6-9 is a banquet—the wedding supper of the Lamb? This will be a meal at which believers from every nation on earth will gather to celebrate God's final work of salvation and the restoration of man to full relationship with God. Notice that it will be a celebration that brings people together. That's what God intended the food in the garden to do in the first place—bring Adam and Eve together around the generous provision of God. Jesus, the sacrificial Lamb of God who was offered for the sin of the world, is Himself the Bread of Life. He is our most satisfying meal and the Meal that will bring all of redeemed humanity together! Food matters.

Food Nurtures
Ladies, just because your husband is an adult doesn't mean his desire to feel the warmth of nurture has disappeared. Twenty-one years of age is not a magic number that makes the need for nurture suddenly vanish into thin air. We men are designed to receive nurturing from our mothers even in the womb, but the need lasts for a lifetime. By nurture I mean the need to feel encouraged, cherished, and cared for. All human beings, no matter what age and stage of life, are in need those things. Being a "grown man" doesn't make what many consider a childhood need disappear. Needing nurture doesn't make him a "mama's boy." That makes him human—someone who is designed and created in the image of God.

What sexual intimacy provides in marriage after the wedding day and companionship provides during courting and marriage, food well-presented provides for men of all ages. It makes men feel regarded, thought of, and valued. David's son Amnon preyed deceitfully upon his sister Tamar's innocence and honorable spirit toward him (2 Samuel 13:1-22). Feigning sickness, his one request was for a meal prepared by his half-sister Tamar. Sadly, he used the cover of sickness to rape her. But her readiness to prepare a meal for her sick brother speaks not only of her kindness, it also speaks of her virtue as a young woman. She was honored to serve him in the tradition their day. Women often prepared the evening meal after their men returned to their work duties following a brief afternoon meal. The preparation often including getting water from the local well and going to the market to buy vegetables from local vendors.

God's intended goal of a mother's nurture was to help her son experience relational wholeness. Wholeness involves the blessing of giving and receiving. It includes knowing how to appreciate the valuable place of and need for women in our lives and humbly recognizing the experience of feeling loved. It absolutely does not mean that "a woman's place is in the kitchen." That's a degrading, arrogant, and unacceptable posture. It simply means that food has a way of helping a man be in touch with his deepest needs, which include recognizing the valuable place of the woman who expresses regard for him by preparing a good meal. Amnon was clearly too selfish to value Tamar's dignity as she had.

Any man, whether he was healthily nurtured by a mother or a mother figure, will continue to have a space in his soul that needs to feel nurtured. I can't tell you exactly why this is so, but God has allowed the satisfaction from food warmly, lovingly, thoughtfully, and tastefully presented by a woman to a man, to speak to a deep need in a man's life.

A man who doesn't feel nurtured with the blessing of food, particularly from his wife, may gradually grow cynical and eventually resentful. "Don't you even care about me?" "Why won't you learn to cook?" If the way to a man's heart is still through his stomach, then someone else could be closer to that destination than you. And that will cause a problem in your relationship. Is the man you love and who has been assigned to your life starving emotionally because you question the wisdom of feeding him physically? Wouldn't it be just like Satan to destroy your relationship with your husband or your son over a plate of food? He destroyed Adam and Eve's intimacy over a simple piece of food. He destroyed Esau and Jacob's relationship over … food. And yet, some of God's greatest miracles in the Bible, performed to show His unconditional love for His people, happened around … food! Ladies, I wonder how you would feel, if the woman who will marry or has married your son chooses to withhold the nurture of making meals that he needs to be physically and relationally healthy?

The preparation of meals has a prominent presence in the Bible … Daniel 1 … Psalm 23 … Amnon wanted Tamar to bring him a meal … It's a symbol of connection, sacrifice, service, honor, endorsement of and value of another … The Wedding Supper of the Lamb … 7 Feasts in the Bible

What's Wrong With His Hands
If I Kill It, Will You Cook It
Thank You For Thinking of Me, For Me
The Necessity of Nurture

(Note: Hannah didn't leave Samuel at the temple until after she had weened him … Miriam brought Moses daily to be fed by his mother)

Food Welcomes

In the Middle Eastern culture, much like southern culture in the U.S., a meal is a big deal. I witnessed it first hand on a trip to Israel in 2013. The food and the hospitality were both amazing! I have witnessed the same phenomenon in America, having grown up in the south, in Virginia. More specifically, I witness it every time I go to visit my mom. If she knows I'm coming home, her first question is, "What can I cook for you guys?" Sometimes I don't tell her I'm coming because I know she'll spend hours preparing amazing southern cuisine or anything else I want to eat—broiled salmon, fried chicken, smothered pork chops, rice and gravy, black-eyed peas, cornbread, collard greens, cabbage, fresh fruit, upside-down pineapple cake, pound cake. You get my point? The list is endless. Whatever Mom thinks her guests, not just her son, want to eat, she makes it happen. Her hospitable spirit wouldn't have it any other way. It's how she welcomes us into her home.

I'll never forget the first time my girlfriend, who is now my wife, came with me to visit at my mother's home in Virginia. We came through the door and found that my mom wasn't home. She was out showing homes for her real estate business. No problem. I went to the kitchen—my usual first stop in the house. I looked on the stove and there was nothing there—not a single pot. The look on my face nearly floored my girlfriend! "What is wrong with you?" she asked. "Are you really pouting because your mother didn't cook?" That question alone almost ended our dating relationship.

How could she not know? I thought to myself. *I never come home without Mom having prepared some of my favorite foods.* To my relief, I discovered that the food was being kept warm in the oven—just for me. Mom hadn't forgotten to welcome me home!

The practice of welcoming people with food goes all the way back to biblical days. In Judges 16, Gideon welcomed a stranger who had come to visit him with a message from God. The message that the LORD was with Gideon and that he would defeat Israel's nemesis, the Midianites, overwhelmed him. Gideon wanted proof that it was God who was speaking, so he offered to bring a meal to Him, if it was Him. He prepared a goat, some bread, and some broth. When it was prepared, Gideon brought it out and the messenger instructed him to lay the meat and the bread on a rock and to pour out the broth. Immediately the items were consumed by a flash of fire! Gideon didn't know it was the angel of the LORD, an Old Testament appearance of Jesus, which theologians call a *theophany*. When the offering of food was consumed, Gideon was sure he would be struck dead. This was his reaction in Judges 6:22 (NIV): "When Gideon realized that it was the angel of the LORD, he exclaimed, 'Alas, Sovereign LORD! I have seen the angel of the LORD face to face!'" Then came this reply in the next verse: "But the Lord said to him, 'Peace! Do not be afraid. You are not going to die.'"

Gideon had welcomed the messenger. But what's more, the messenger, who was revealed to be God, had welcomed Gideon and his offering!

In the Bible food is often a symbol of welcome, *shalom* (peace), and oneness. A meal prepared for anyone is a powerful sign of peace between the preparer and the recipient and a gesture of togetherness that cannot be disputed. We've seen this truth not only when we open our home to friends, family, and strangers with a meal; we've also seen it played out with neighbors recently. Augie and Maggie are wonderful neighbors and very kind people. For more than thirteen years we've waved hello and goodbye and exchanged pleasantries. Augie is a tool guy. There is not a tool that he doesn't have in his garage. So when I've needed help with a home project (Trust me. It's never huge.) he's been my guy.

The unique thing about our relationship is that we've never spent time in each other's homes. Augie made his aversion to hospitality clear the week we moved in. He greeted us warmly, but he added, "I'm not the kind who will have his feet under your table." *No problem,* I thought. *We'll stay out of your way.* Initially I was uncertain whether his remark was racial in nature. They're white. Our family is African American, and we were the only ones in the neighborhood at the time. But we've always had a warm and cordial relationship with sometimes extended conversations on the lawn—but not at the dinner table.

Fast forward thirteen years. Augie came by to tell us that Maggie had a rare form of cancer and had elected to forgo chemotherapy and other damaging treatments because it was not likely they will help her. Sheri and I stopped by to visit Maggie and to pray with her. For nearly two hours we talked, laughed, and looked at their family photos. The one thing Maggie said to us was, "I'm mostly concerned about Augie." My wife in her wisdom replied, "We'll look out for him and bring him food to keep him going."

Well wouldn't you know it! Those wonderful meals of smothered pork chops, ribs, greens, and my wife's secret cornbread (Augie's favorite) have taken our relationship to another level. We've sat for hours talking as Maggie has continued to decline. Augie comes by and chats—still on the doorstep, but I think the kitchen table is coming soon. He's a kind but very independent person. But when a good meal comes from the Hairston home, I've seen him melt like butter.

You see, what makes all this really special is that we've been praying for Augie to come to faith in Jesus for thirteen years! On my most recent visit to deliver food, Maggie who is a Christian, said to me, "Rod, you're a real Christian. I really mean that. You guys are so kind and thoughtful. We don't know how to say thank you." "No thanks needed, Maggie," I said. "We're praying for you. Pray with us that Augie will say yes to Jesus." Sheri and I believe Jesus is not only going to welcome Maggie home into heaven soon. We're asking him to use something as simple as meals shared to help us introduce Augie to Christ so he can be welcomed home someday as well.

So what does all of that have to do with your marriages, ladies? Food is a powerful way of making your husband feel especially welcomed by you and welcomed into the home you both share. Try welcoming him home regularly with a meal that's been prepared with him in mind. Let me know what impact it has on him.

Food Honors

In Matthew 22, Jesus spoke of a king inviting preferred guests to a wedding feast. The wedding feast represented a special and customary celebration of marriage between the king's son and his bride. In this parable, Jesus is both the King and the Son. The preferred guests are the Jews who rejected the King and His Son.

One thing that should also be noted in this parable is that the first rejection of the invitation was looked over and a second sent. With the second invitation, Jesus highlights the menu. "Again, he sent out other servants, saying, 'Tell those who are invited, "See, I have prepared my dinner; my oxen and fatted cattle are killed, and all things are ready. Come to the wedding."' But they made light of it and went their ways, one to his own farm, another to his business" (Matthew 22:4-5). The food detail expresses the level of sacrifice involved in the preparation of the meal.

The guests should clearly have known that they were being treated with deference and honor as those with a special place in the King's heart. Why else would the King extend such a significant invitation? These guests were *first*, as Jesus was sent "first to the house of the lost sheep of Israel" (Matthew 15:24). They were the priority of the King. What an honored position to hold!

The food in this wonderful passage was a tool to express honor and priority. It was prepared for the King's special guests, who were on His A-list. The word *dinner* means, literally, "best meal." The wedding feast represents a special meal, specially prepared for the evening celebration. Ladies, the point is not that men need a wedding feast every evening. The point is that special meals can speak honor to a man. They can tell a man that he's on your A-List and that he holds a special place in your heart and has been specially invited. And yes, for him to show up late or not hungry or not at all would be terribly disappointing to you, just as it was for the King who laid out his best meal for his guests. And just as it will be for this same King if we don't attend the feast where He has laid out His best meal for us.

Chapter 7 Reflections:

1. Food was important to our human experience in Bible times, and it's important now. The question that we must ask and answer is, "Why do men tend to want women to cook for them?" I bet you've been wondering the same thing, especially if you're not particularly fond of cooking.

2. What sexual intimacy provides in marriage after the wedding day and companionship provides during courting and marriage, food well-presented does for men of all ages. It makes men feel regarded, thought of, and valued.

3. I can't tell you exactly why this is so, but God has allowed the satisfaction from food warmly, lovingly, thoughtfully, and tastefully presented by a woman to a man, to speak to a deep need in a man's life.

8

Assist Him
He May Be Capable, But No Man Can Do It All Alone

It's true … mostly. Men don't like to ask for help, and we'd rather find our way than ask for directions. I think it's built into us. We relish the challenge and the accomplishment. Getting it done on our own and finding our way are sort of badges of honor. It's all part of a broken *man code* that says, "Don't ask for help. Be a man and handle it yourself."

It is well-documented that men are less likely to visit our family doctors than women are. More women get skin cancer, but more men die from it because we are slow to seek medical attention. The rates of suicide among men in the U.S. is four times higher than it is among women. Among the leading causes are the breakdown of relationships, social isolation, and inability to form and sustain meaningful relationships. Men need help, but we're really slow to seek it.

Admittedly, that is not the best or wisest approach to life. And yes, we do let our pride get in the way. But work with us ladies; we usually mean well. It's not all about big egos. Some of it is our bent toward conquest. It is a man thing—that thing in us that likes to figure it out alone, work until we conquer the challenge, or climb the ladder with no one to hold it. In our minds, we can handle it. It's no big deal. But we're not always right, and sometimes we're not even in our right minds! We do need your help.

Ladies, we not only need your help, we want your help. I'm saying that for the men in your life because they may not always say it: We need you. We need your help. We need your support. We need your assistance.

There's only one caveat. We need you to help us without making a big deal of it. Can you help us without a reminding us how silly we are to not ask? Can you help us without a tongue-lashing, without shaming, without making us finally admit that you were right? (We already know you're right.) Will you help willingly and joyfully? That will not only make your man's day; it will also, eventually, make him more likely to ask you and more likely to appreciate the precious gift he has in you.

I can attest that oftentimes when men are working, words get in the way. Whether it's writing, cutting, lifting, pulling, measuring, or driving, fewer words are usually more helpful. More words tend to be less helpful. Yes, there are exceptions, but if a man is focused on a task, he's usually not interested in talking or hearing someone else talk. Have you ever noticed how two men lifting a heavy object keep their conversations to the bare minimum—"Turn left. Steady. Watch your step. Right there. Done." It's not personal that he won't ask for help or talk to you while you're working together. It's just a guy thing. We're literally wired for fewer words, and sometimes that works to our disadvantage. We don't use them when we really need them—i.e., when it's time to ask for support.

He Needs Your Help

Sisters, I have undeniable proof that your man needs your help. I don't need a survey, and I don't really need statistics to prove it to you. I know your husband needs your help because God designed him to need help. God didn't make Adam in such a way that he could flourish on his own. He didn't make him in such a way that he could live his best life as an uber-independent man. After He created Adam on the sixth day, "God saw everything that He had made, and indeed it was very good" (Genesis 1:31). Adam was good. God did not make a mistake. But Adam's relationship status was not good.

God gave Adam authority to name the animals. But dominion over the beasts of the field—the ability to tame wild broncos, kiss lions, and ride the backs of bisons—was not a fix for his aloneness. God's solution to Adam's relationship status was not more work with longer hours to complete his tasks. It was, "I will make him a *helper* comparable to him" (Genesis 2:18 italics mine). Ladies, Adam was no good by himself. So God made a helper "comparable to" or "suitable for" him.

Let's be clear. God doesn't make anything unnecessarily. He is not in the business of experimenting with His creation. He's too perfect for that. Everything God creates has purpose and usefulness in His program. He is the impeccable Matchmaker, making perfect complements for everything that needs one. For the left foot God made a right foot. To complement the left ear, God made the right ear. For the man He created, God made a female complement who has exactly the helping capacity that Adam needs. Ladies, you have something that your Adam can't succeed without. You have inestimable value. You are more necessary than most men will admit. A man's world is incomplete without your gifts, strengths, acumen, abilities, intelligence, emotions, and insights.

I don't think Adam fully understood himself until Eve was delivered to him. Likewise, a man won't really recognize himself until he embraces his Eve. When God brought Eve to Adam, he responded with understandable joy and excitement. But I believe Adam's response is also an indication of perhaps his most admirable character quality: humility. He humbly accepted both his helper and the fact that he needed help.

Life in the garden, before sin entered, must have been an amazing symbiosis of love, respect, mutual admiration, and teamwork. Adam knew himself—who he was, why he was, and what he was capable of—because he welcomed Eve into his life as his helper. He knew she was God's gift to him. Without complaining, he accepted his limitations, though he was crystal clear about his strengths. He loved his helper-wife and celebrated her place in his life because in the sin-free garden, Adam loved himself. Remember what the apostle Paul said: "he who loves his wife loves himself. For no one ever hated his own flesh, but nourishes and cherishes it, just as the Lord does the church" (Ephesians 5:28b-29). Before sin's devastating impact, there was no place for what later came to be known as male pride or male *insecurity*. Adam humbly admitted his need for Eve's help, and he welcomed it.

Needing Help Is Hard

We may be several thousands of years from the garden of Eden, but ladies, men still need help. The only difference now is that sin has ruined those perfectly harmonious dynamics between husband and wife that Adam and Eve shared. The days of being naked and unashamed are long gone. One bite of the forbidden fruit and needing help suddenly became difficult. Now insecurities, shame, fears of feeling exposed, and rifts in our intimacy get in the way. Vulnerability can be like Superman's kryptonite. It makes men feel weak, and we don't like that. We don't like looking or feeling needy and inadequate. The voice of shame whispers to us, "I thought you were a real man. Can't you do that little thing by yourself?" It tells us we shouldn't need your help or anyone else's. Or at least, we shouldn't have to always ask. Yes, it's complicated.

My stepfather, whom we called Pop, was the only real grandfather my kids ever knew. He and my mom were married for twenty-six years. His thirty-year navy career, from 1965 to 1994, took him across the seven seas to places I could only imagine—the Bering Strait, the Black Sea, Egypt, Saudi Arabia—the list goes on and on. He was a rarity among his peers, having achieved the rank of Master Chief as an African American during years of extraordinary racism in the military. What got him through was an impeccable work ethic and commitment to his craft. Master Chief Boyd, as he was often called, was a man's man. He was direct, gruff, no-nonsense, and loyal to his friends.

When heart failure began to take its toll on his health, I saw a side to life as a man that's worth noting. You see, Pop was really clear about needing his wife, my mom. Rarely did he cook; he'd just sit and wait until she came home. After he retired from the Navy and took a security contractor position, he'd call my Mom several times a day, "just to check in." He missed her while she worked and longed for her to be where he was. He needed her, but I never once heard him say it. And she enjoyed the fact that he needed her. Together they had special rhythm.

The more his health deteriorated, the more he fought to maintain his manly independence. When the doctors could do nothing else for him, they suggested hospice care at home. He totally refused. He made the medical equipment company remove the medical bed from their home because as he said, "I'm going to sleep in my own bed." He refused a wheel chair and only gave in to having a walker because Mom demanded it.

Though he was extremely weak, he was determined to get around the house on foot with his heart and medication monitor in tow. Walking put him at risk for a fall, but he mustered the strength to grab the hand rail and laboriously conquered every step to the second floor (especially when my brothers and I were around). Pop was set on going upstairs and downstairs under his own strength. Of course, he needed my mom or someone else to keep a hand on his back. But in his mind, he was doing it on his own.

The night before Master Chief Boyd, Pop, went to be with Jesus in heaven, he climbed the stairs of their home one more time, Mom said. I think he knew it was his last time. And I think he did it just to make it clear: "I can still do it by myself." Pop needed a lot of help as he neared the end of his life. That last climb, like all the previous ones, was made with the support of my mom and my auntie. They gladly aided him, even as he grunted, "I got it!" As it is for most men, needing the help was always hard for him, even till his last day.

For the man He created, God made a female complement who has exactly the helping capacity that Adam needs. Ladies, you have something that your Adam can't succeed without. You have inestimable value. You are more necessary than most men will admit. A man's world is incomplete without your gifts, strengths, acumen, abilities, intelligence, emotions, and insights.

You ask, "Why?" It's because most we men don't want to be a burden to anyone, including to the women we love. It may seem over the top and silly to a woman, but needing help is hard for men—even when it's obvious to you that we need it.

He Needs You to Want To

So what's the secret? How do you get a man to admit he needs help and to ask for it? Vulnerability is easier where there's closeness and security. For a man to experience the feeling that comes with being vulnerable is unsettling. We resist it immediately and slip quickly back into lone-wolf mode. What comes with vulnerability is the fear that we will be judged— judged for needing, judged for not knowing, judged for not being capable. We know that no one knows everything, but it's the emotional exposure that comes with not knowing that makes men less given to asking for help.

And truthfully, though you don't mean to, sometimes wives make it difficult for men to ask for help. Snide remarks, deep sighs of frustration, past displays of irritation, impatience with our process, rolling eyes, or just simple busyness are all suggestions that our need for your help is a burden.

The feeling of being judged as inadequate comes with all of that. And it discourages vulnerability and deeper relational closeness.

So how does a man get to a place where he's comfortable with vulnerability and asking for help? That happens when he knows, more and more, that you want to be his Eve—his "helper suitable." The more you celebrate his small wins and his imperfect efforts, the more he knows and feels that you're for him. It tells him you're in it with him—whatever he's working on. Gently offer to help him: "Is there anything I can do to help you, honey?" "Can I bring you something cold to drink?" "Do you need anything?" "I'm here if you need me." Sometimes just having you sitting in the same room where he's working is a huge show of support. Sometimes all it takes is just the fact that you offered. If he asks for the slightest bit of help, words like, "I'm happy to do that for you" help him to let down his guard. They let him know you're his Eve and that you're delighted to be that person in his life.

It takes time and consistency before a man becomes convinced that his woman genuinely wants to be a support to him. His slowness to come around is not necessarily your fault. We're all still trying to recover closeness from the fall in the garden. When Adam ate the fruit Eve handed him, there was instant separation between the two of them and between them and God. God's search-and-rescue mission came with the clarion question, "Adam, where are you?" It wasn't that God couldn't find Adam. He knew exactly where Adam was—hiding in his nakedness. All of a sudden, exposure and vulnerability became a thing for the man. When God asked Adam, "Who told you that you were naked?" the distance between Adam and Eve became instantly, apparent: "The woman you gave me ...." Blame, emotional distance, and suspicion have since entered the equations of our marriages. And overcoming them requires constant intentionality.

Here is a list of some practical ways to build closeness with the man you've dedicated your life to and to assure him that you want to be the helper God designed you to be:

- Focus on his strengths. We all have weaknesses, and they don't have to be ignored. But focusing on his strengths lets him know you see the best in him.

- Celebrate his strengths to others, especially to your kids and your girlfriends. A man knows when he is honored among his children and your friends. If he feels dishonored by your conversations and comments to others, it'll be a long time before he can open up and need you.
- When he invites your support, be sure to follow through. Otherwise he'll go back to the failed mantra that says, "If you want something done and done right, you have to do it yourself." Remember, consistency builds confidence and confidence grows closeness.
- Tell him thank you for what he does, even if he hasn't welcomed your help yet. (If what he's doing alone is dangerous or life-threatening, certainly appeal to him to take a different approach. Let him know you'd like to keep him around—alive.) Let him know you'd love to help by sharing a meaningful portion of the load.

When you take those sorts of practical steps with a tone of honor, your man will never be able to deny that you *want to* assist him on the journey of life. Experience and Scripture guarantee that both of you will enjoy a more fulfilling relationship together. You'll have a thriving partnership and camaraderie that will keep the devil at bay, Jesus at the center, and the two of you closer to one another.

Chapter 8 Reflections:
1. It is a man thing—that thing in us that likes to figure it out alone, work until we conquer the challenge, or climb the ladder with no one to hold it. In our minds, we can handle it. It's no big deal. But we're not always right, and sometimes we're not even in our right minds! We do need your help.

2. For the man He created, God made a female complement who has exactly the helping capacity that Adam needs. Ladies, you have something that your Adam can't succeed without. You have inestimable value. You are more necessary than most men will admit. A man's world is incomplete without your gifts, strengths, acumen, abilities, intelligence, emotions, and insights.

3. The more you celebrate his small wins and his imperfect efforts, the more he knows and feels that you're for him. It tells him you're in it with him—whatever he's working on. Gently offer to help him: "Is there anything I can do to help you, honey?"

9

Prioritize Him
Show Him He Fits Into Your Life Scheme

Every man likes to feel that he matters—that he's important—if only to one person. Ladies, your man may not have articulated this to you, but he needs to matter to you. It's not one of those things men talk about … until, of course, it's not happening. Even then, we usually just pout—in silent withdrawal. Whether in the intimacy of the marriage relationship or a serious dating relationship, we men want to know that we're at the top of your to-do list and principal among your considerations.

Of course, women desire the same thing. It's human. It's consistent with what the noted American psychologist Abraham Maslow called our need for love and belonging. Wherever you place the need on Maslow's hierarchy, we all have it. But ladies, I think we can agree that most women will openly make the need known—the need to feel loved, to feel wanted, to be connected, to matter to someone. Not men. The thought of articulating the need to be a priority in your life and in your daily schedule makes him feel awkward, weak, and vulnerable. That doesn't negate the fact, however, that your man is less irritable and grumbly when he feels that he's a priority to you.

If you're married to your Boaz … or your Joe or Jim or Harry, take this chapter seriously. Men show up at work every day with an often-unspoken frustration: "Everything and everyone else in her life are more important than I am. Her work, her boss, her girlfriends, her Netflix shows, her workouts, her diet, the children, the book club, Facebook, Instagram, and Twitter." I've heard men joke with other guys: "At least your wife greets you at the door! My wife is never home when I come through the door. And when she is, all I get is, "Hey! I'm upstairs. What do you want to do for dinner?"

Ladies, he may have a tough time finding the words to tell you that he wants to be your priority. But it will not be hard for him to enjoy the feeling of being a priority to a female co-worker who thinks he's the smartest, funniest, most attractive man in the office. Her morning greeting, her smile, and her offer to grab him lunch while she's out may be innocent, but it will fill an empty space in his life that he's never had the courage to discuss with you.

If the notion of prioritizing your man is overwhelming or uninviting, prayerfully consider this biblical principle: "Give and it will come back to you, with good measure, pressed down, shaken together and running over will be put into your bosom" (Luke 6:38). Because we all want to be the priority of the person we love, making him, his needs, and his desires first on our list will have a wonderful boomerang effect. The law of reciprocity always comes into play in our relationships. Positive reciprocity is always better than negative reciprocity when it comes to the people we love and care about the most. Here are some practical things you can do.

Action Speaks

Leadership guru, author, and business leader John Maxwell says that action is what separates great people from mediocre people. In other words, people who take action grow, change, reach lofty goals, and attain success in life. In other words, "we become what we do." If you want to become a bodybuilder, weight training must be high on your to-do list. Many people want to become writers. It's a wonderful aspiration, and they have plenty of helpful insights to share with people. But you only become a writer if you ... yes, write. John Maxwell writes every day, which explains why he's such a prolific author. Action is the crucial link between our ideas and our outcomes, what we desire and our reality. Whatever a person does consistently is what a person becomes.

If you want your man to know that he's the priority in your life, there are some actions both of you have to take. Some of those actions depend on the person and his needs. Others make sense for any marriage. For example, it's difficult to maintain oneness without regularly spending gratifying time together. It's easy for a month or even months to pass by without having enjoyed a delicious meal out together, a performance at the opera house, a picnic in the park, or a walk down memory lane while looking through old family photos. It may be challenging to get him to slow down without too much coercion, but tell him you got him tickets to see his favorite music group or reservations at his favorite restaurant and see what happens.

Sometime prioritizing him involves taking unpleasant tasks off his plate. Schedule to have a car detailer come to the house over the weekend. Ask him if he has a list of clothing needs that you can shop for. Personally, I like to shop for my own, but I feel special whenever Sheri picks up my dry cleaning.

I asked my wife, "What are some things you do to make me feel like a priority?" I had to ask because I knew there was no way I could keep track of all the amazing things she does habitually. It's absolutely rare that I feel I'm playing second fiddle to something or someone in Sheri's life. But this has been a growth area in our marriage. None of this has happened overnight. It has taken lots of time, prayer, hurt feelings, frustrations, forgiveness, listening, forgetting, and trying again—on both our parts. It's that way for any good relationship because it requires that we posture ourselves as learners in order understand what's important to the other person.

Peter gave this admonition to husbands when he said, "Husbands, likewise, dwell with them with understanding, giving honor to the wife, as to the weaker vessel, and as being heirs together of the grace of life, that your prayers may not be hindered" (1 Peter 3:7). The charge is to husbands, but the principle plays out for wives as well. It calls both spouses to work at knowing their life partner more deeply and more intimately. Ladies, do you know what your man needs, what makes him tick, and what makes him feel that he's tops on your list of tasks?

When I asked my wife how she prioritizes me, I was amazed at how well she really does know me. She knows that I need support for my many travels, so she tries to keep my shirts rotated at the dry cleaners. She knows I like to snack on a certain kind of chip and a certain kind of nut, so she tries to keep me supplied. She's aware of the non-alcoholic beers that I enjoy drinking when I'm winding down. And even when she sees that my tastes are shifting, she said, "I just adjust and try to anticipate your needs." She knows that order in my study and living spaces at home calm me, so she keeps an eye out so I can relax or get right to my work if necessary. She keeps an eye out for my brand of deodorant and the toothpastes I like, making sure I have a fresh supply when they're low. If my medications are running low, because I'm her priority, she delights to pick them up for me at the pharmacy before I run out.

As I listened to her response to my question, I was overwhelmed with how much my woman loves her man. I was also impressed with how in-tune she has become with my emotional needs over the years. Sheri is zeroed in on me. No one else knows me the way she does. No one feeds my heart the way she does. I tell her all the time, "You have a full-time job prioritizing me. I'm a real high-need kind of dude." She just smiles and says, "It's my honor." Ladies, no one else should know your man the way you do. And he should be no one's greatest priority besides yours.

> *Because we all want to be the priority of the person we love, making him, his needs, and his desires first on our list will have a wonderful boomerang effect. The law of reciprocity always comes into play in our relationships.*

A final word on this matter of actions that speak: No one can serve another, especially a spouse, without the help of the Holy Spirit. He is the one who gives us more capacity to love, to be patient, to extend grace, to be gentle, to do good. Check out the fruit of the Spirit:

> But the Holy Spirit produces this kind of fruit in our lives: love, joy, peace, patience, kindness, goodness, faithfulness, gentleness, and self-control. There is no law against these things!" (Galatians 5:22-23)

I'd hate for you to get the impression that prioritizing your man is easy. He might be a really disagreeable or unkind person. You may be growing weary trying to figure out how to be the woman God wants you to be in his life. Prayer and the power of the Holy Spirit are the keys. That's what my wife tells me. And she should know. She's had me to deal with for nearly thirty years!

Kids Come Second

It often comes as a shock to young couples who are early in the childbearing and childrearing years of their marriages when Sheri and I say, "You've got to put the kids second." We tell young parents and sometimes more seasoned parents that kids have to be a welcomed addition to the family, but they can't be allowed to run the family. For that matter, they can't be allowed to run or ruin the marriage.

In the excitement of becoming a new parent and experiencing the joy and blessing of a lifetime—a new baby boy or girl—something very important can get lost. Most often, moms lose sight of the needs and place of their husbands. I've counseled countless men who struggled with feelings of confusion and abandonment. They were confused because they too love their new addition to the family. How could something so wonderful make them feel so displaced in their own homes and marriages? When children become the home's priority, men start to feel abandoned by their spouses and resentment begins to grow.

Studies have also shown that thoroughly involved fathers also experience a dip in their testosterone levels when a child is born. It correlates with the mother's estrogen levels. It's possible for both to experience some degree of postpartum depression. Feeling relationally and emotionally disconnect from his spouse, who may be highly and narrowly focused on the baby, only exacerbates the matter. What should be a joyous though demanding transition in the family can become a source of deep frustration.

If your husband feels that he has to compete for your attention, either because of a newborn or because of teenagers who garner all your energy and attention, he may stop seeking it. When that happens, his need for attention—the need to feel like he's your first priority—will be addressed some other way. It's quite possible he will turn to something healthy to get the attention he needs. What that could be, I have no idea. More likely, loneliness will make him not only resentful, but also vulnerable to an emotional or sexual affair.

You can be a great mom, give the kids the attention they need, and still prioritize your husband without adding stress or hours to your day. The kids will not only be fine, they will feel more secure. Your closeness to your husband is a message to the kids that all is well and home is good. Kids of all ages almost always fight having a bedtime. Especially when they're newborns or toddlers, they don't always like it when you lay them down.

But they absolutely survive it. They've done so for ages. You'll be back to pick them up, feed them, and change them, before they know it. Work out a schedule and a routine. But whatever you do, give your man some quality, focused attention, regularly. Both of you will enjoy the kids more together. And when the kids are grown up and long-gone, you and your hubby will still be going strong.

Of course, there can be unique circumstances. More and more families are trying to juggle the dynamics of two parents with careers, children with special needs, social demands, church life, and more. Try to keep your eyes on the big picture. When it's all said and done, what will matter if everything is stripped away? I've always imagined what I will say to Jesus when I stand before Him someday. "Sorry my schedule was always out of control." "No, I didn't pray about whether I should've joined that club." "Yes, I wish I had worked harder at loving Sheri, but the kids and the ministry needed me." I don't think any of that's going to fly. You get the idea, moms?

I'm not trying to make a case that your marriage is more important than your kids. Okay, actually I am. Not in a narrow way though, but as a matter of order. God is a God of order. He places Christ as the head of the husband and the husband as the head of his wife. Scripture always places the children under the parents—last in the family chain (See Psalm 128, 1 Corinthians 11:3, Ephesians 6:1-4). Last certainly doesn't mean insignificant or of little worth. It simply reflects the order of emphasis. But many parents jack up the order, putting the kids before their spouses, and wonder why their home lives are chaotic, unharmonious, and unruly.

Trust God on this one, ladies. Your children will be just fine if you put your husband first. But I can't guarantee your marriage will not suffer if you put your children ahead of your husband. You could be putting both your marriage and your family in danger if the order is wrong.

Calendar Items

Seventy years are given to us!
Some even live to eighty.
But even the best years are filled with pain and trouble;
soon they disappear, and we fly away.

Who can comprehend the power of your anger?
Your wrath is as awesome as the fear you deserve.
Teach us to realize the brevity of life,
so that we may grow in wisdom.
(Psalm 90:10-12 NLT)

Life is short and time flies by quickly. As I write this chapter, my wife sits across the room from me. It's Valentine's Day, the day of love, and she has allowed me the morning to write before we go out and have some fun together. I'm amazed that over thirty years have gone by so quickly. Last night on our way to do some shopping for a big trip we have planned together, she reminded me that my first Valentine to her was delivered by my mom … of all people! That's a long story. But the point is this. The time has flown by. When we began dating in 1987, I was twenty-one years old and she was eighteen.

In Psalm 90, Moses offers us some brilliant wisdom for managing our priorities: "Teach us to realize the brevity of life, so that we may grow in wisdom." In the ESV the first sentence reads, "Teach us to number our days …." At fifty-two, I'm learning to number my days. I'm learning to count them carefully and to be careful to make them count. They go by so quickly that I can't afford to waste a single one. As the adage goes, "Once it's gone, you can't get it back."

To *number our days* means to count them, to allot them, to weigh them out, or to appoint them. The idea is to be judicious and intentional about how we use them. To do that means I have to plan my days, including what I'm going to do, how, where, when, and with whom. We don't have to plan every minute of every day. But we certainly have to consider the hours, the activities, and the theme of each day.

Ladies, numbering our days means that whoever is a priority in our lives must be factored into our day … on purpose. That may sound sort of rigid and mechanical. It doesn't have to be. But I've found it to be true that what I put on my calendar and my to-do list is much more likely to get my time and my attention. Every day, I try to make a to-do list that includes my work, my personal chores, and my marriage. Somethings don't need to go on a calendar for me. I try to spend time with God every morning—reading, praying, listening. I try to spend time stimulating my thinking every day by reading. And I try to spend time daily connecting with Sheri. Sometimes it's over a cup of coffee in the morning. Some days it's over lunch or dinner together.

Sheri is an item on my daily calendar. And because it's been that way for a long time, I don't really have to write it on my calendar any more. In the past I did. That helped me develop the habit of making her a priority on purpose. I encourage you to do the same thing for your man. Make your relationship with him an item on your calendar every day. Whatever you think will be a meaningful way of prioritizing him, add it to your calendar.

Now, let me alert you. He probably won't notice it right away. We guys can be a little slow that way. And truthfully, we're much less relational than women are, generally speaking. Yep, we are often clueless. You will probably feel taken for granted and unappreciated in the process. Hold your water, as they say. Don't get discouraged. Don't let his failure to acknowledge your efforts (even though he should acknowledge your efforts) cause you to regret what you're doing. Just add him as an item on your calendar and talk to God about it. God sees and "[He] is not unjust to forget your work and labor of love which you have shown toward His name" (Hebrews 6:10 ESV).

Remember, as you put your man on your calendar, you are prioritizing him. And when you prioritize him, you're covering him. I'm confident God will honor your efforts.

Goal-Setting

A final word about learning how to prioritize your man. Priorities are a function of goals. Goals are simply our desired outcomes and what we will pursue to make them happen. Goals are always challenged by interruptions—like this wonderful iPhone X that won't stop ringing while I'm writing. The only reason I haven't turned it off is because I told my wife to call me when she's ready for me to pick her up from her Valentine's Day spa gift. Otherwise, I should turn it off because it's getting in the way of my goal to complete this book.

Are you tracking with me? Goals determine priorities. What goals do you have for your relationship with the man of you love? The two of you may have goals together, but you can also have goals of your own related to covering him. Maybe you have a goal to make him feel so affirmed and confident that he will never second-guess himself again. May you have a goal to cover him with so much prayer that he will always feel the power and presence of God working in his business. Maybe you have a goal to make home a remarkable haven of rest for him.

Every year I spend time establishing my goals for the year. Once I've prayed about them and allowed God to sift them, separating the ones that are Spirit-led from the ones that are driven by my flesh, I begin the process of putting action items on my calendar. That allows me to keep my goals in front of me rather than in a hidden document that I may never look at again. It also presses me to act on my goals.

Acting on goals is the hardest and the most fun part of achieving them. And that's the point. Anything you want to change, accomplish, or obtain needs goals. Of course, we know that all of our goal-setting still needs the help and power of God. Achieving our goals is not only up to us. Proverbs 16:9 is one of my favorite goals-and-planning Scriptures: "A man's heart plans his way, / But the Lord directs his steps."

Many people get the heart of that verse wrong. The writer is not saying, "There's no need to plan because God's going to do whatever God wants to do." Quite the opposite. He's reminding us that God has nothing to direct if we don't make plans! In other words, our plans are the material God often uses to bring about our miracles. He uses our plans and introduces us to the people who will help us accomplish them. I wonder how many miracles we've missed because we had no plan, giving Him no direction to act in on our behalf. I wonder how many divine contacts we may have ignored—people who would have advocated for us and given toward our dreams—because we had no plan. Goals and plans matter to God. Try sharing your Spirit-led goals for covering your husband with God. As you remain diligent toward them, expect to see God's blessing on your relationship. He says, "The plans of the diligent lead surely to plenty" (Proverbs 21:5 NLT). Eugene Peterson, in his paraphrase of the Bible called *The Message*, renders the verse like this: "Careful planning puts you ahead in the long run." Get ready to get ahead in your connection with your man as you prioritize, set goals, plan, and make him and item on your calendar.

Chapter 9 Reflections:

1. Because we all want to be the priority of the person we love, making him, his needs, and his desires first on our list will have a wonderful boomerang effect. The law of reciprocity always comes into play in our relationships.

2. No one can serve another, especially a spouse, without the help of the Holy Spirit. He is the one who gives us more capacity to love, to be patient, to extend grace, to be gentle, to do good.

3. If your husband feels that he has to compete for your attention, either because of a newborn or because of teenagers who garner all your energy and attention, he may stop seeking it. When that happens, his need for attention—the need to feel like he's your first priority—will be addressed some other way.

10

Paint the Boundaries For Him
Men Need Clear Standards

"I wish she wouldn't let me get away with murder. I like [my girlfriend] because she demands certain things of me." (Anonymous)

This chapter could be called "The Tough-Love Chapter" because every relationship needs a little tough love. The relationships between a woman and her man are no exception. My experience counseling many couples has proven that healthy relationships need clear boundaries that define the limits of what's acceptable and what's not acceptable. Relationships need boundaries that clarify what's loving and respectful and what isn't. Boundaries tell you how far you can go with me and how much I will tolerate from you. They tell us what's ours and what belongs to someone else. Boundaries are a beautiful thing.

Ladies, you cannot accept every behavior, every manner of treatment, every expectation placed on you, or every manner of conversation directed toward you. You cannot—not if you demand to be respected and desire to be loved. You must not because you are made in the image of God, and that means you have extraordinary value!

A man who selfishly transgresses your emotional, physical, spiritual, and financial boundaries is self-absorbed. No amount of pleading, asking, or begging will fix his warped perspectives about love and your relationship. The only thing that will work is unbending, unmoving, and uncompromising boundaries. My wife says, "You have to tell people how to treat you." And a woman's boundaries—the kind that are God-ordained—tell a man how you demand to be treated.

I feel a deep passion about this issue because I've watched so many women allow the men they loved genuinely to treat them poorly. One of the reasons I wrote *Cover Her* was to challenge men to live out the mandate of

God for their lives. We are commanded by God to create a safe place for the ladies in our lives and to see to it that they reach His destiny for them. I wrote it to help women know what they should expect from any man who wants to be in relationship with them. The levels of violence toward women, in our nation and in the world, is staggering and sickening. The disrespect and the belittling have to stop.

What's more, many of the men I've counseled over the years tell me clearly that they prefer a woman who has standards and boundaries. Healthy, confident men respect a woman who respects herself. We identify with the notion of respect because it is a primary operating principle in our lives. God built us in such a way that we prize it, need it, and want it. As Deacon Horace Spady, a dear friend, use to say in his southern, Virginia drawl and his slow, masculine cadence, "You don't have to love me, but *you're gonna respect me!*" I only wish you could hear him the way I hear him in my mind.

Ladies, many men will not respect a woman who allows herself to be treated any kind of way by her man or by anyone else. So when you value and regard yourself with clear boundaries, men know you're not to be taken lightly. Real men respect that. If a man insists on transgressing your boundaries, lose the loser, call the police, walk away, press the charges, put your dog on him, get counseling. I give you permission to take care of yourself! In other words, do whatever it takes short of maiming and murdering him.

Lines, Lanes, and Limits

"For each one shall bear his own load." (Galatians 6:5)

"But let your 'Yes' be 'Yes,' and your 'No,' 'No.' For whatever is more than these is from the evil one." (Matthew 5:37)

The single biggest factor facing our tired and worn-out culture in the U.S. just might be the inability to say no. In a desire to please, to be thought well of, to be nice, to find approval, or to feel needed, we live with no defining lines. We often live in lanes of life that are not sanctioned for us by God. And we often are not good at accepting our own limits. That may explain why many of us are simply burning out and feeling out of control.

It's not just that we're tired. When we become exhausted, resentment and disillusionment begin building. Our perspectives become cloudy. And our fuses start growing dangerously short. Things that were once a joy become undesirable chores and burdens. We are saying yes when we really want to say no. Is this the abundant life Jesus promised? Is this what it means to love God and to love my neighbor?

Ladies, I want to talk to you about lines, lanes, and limits. I've been finding that many women (and men, for that matter) don't know where their own emotional, spiritual, and even physical boundaries are anymore. Sometimes we don't know where we end and where others begin. We're unsure what we're responsible for and what others are responsible for. For the sake of relationship sanity, it's time we get in our lanes and stay in them. It's time we get clear about our limits. It's time to draw some appropriate and necessary lines. It's time we let our "Yes" be "Yes" and our "No" be "No."

> *Many men will not respect a woman who allows herself to be treated any kind of way by her man or by anyone else. So when you value and regard yourself with clear boundaries, men know you're not to be taken lightly. Real men respect that.*

I bet you've discovered that it's impossible to please everyone. Anyone who lives to please too many people will soon become deeply displeased with themselves and their lives. Ladies, you can't please everyone. True. But you also will never be able to please the man you're called to cover all the time. And he's only one person. Let that sink in for your own emotional and spiritual health. You're not responsible to please him or anyone else at all times. We don't even please God all the time. I'm thankful that our failures, sins, and disappointments are covered by the blood of Jesus. Ladies, you need to give yourself what I call *breathing room*.

Breathing room is that space you and I need in order to be fully human. It's the space in our lives where we need to be able to say, "I'm so sorry I can't do that for you today." Breathing room lets you take a break from other's needs, demands, and unreasonable expectations. It's a space filled with grace that allows you to be imperfect and on a journey in life. It lets you figure out how to be fully you, in all of your glory and imperfections. You are "fearfully and wonderfully made" (Psalm 139:14).

Breathing room in our lives, however, gets consumed and depleted when we fail to let others live with their disappointments with us. It gets swallowed up when we fail to let others take responsibility for themselves. To put it another way, husbands and wives are called to cover each other, but we're not responsible for each other's reactions, behaviors, and responsibilities. You will become stifled and anxiety-filled if you try to live according to other people's unfair and unrealistic expectations of you. This is a place to draw a dotted line between you and your husband. Having done your best to cover him, you shouldn't have to carry the weight of making life happen for him. And you should have room to journey in the direction of your God-given dreams while you're also trying to support his. When you lose sight of you and become absorbed in the other person's liabilities, the relationship begins to disintegrate because you're not speaking the truth in love. You begin living with a low-grade resentment that will increase to a boiling temperature unawares.

Drs. Henry Cloud and John Townsend in their groundbreaking book *Boundaries* say, "Many clinical psychological symptoms, such as depression, anxiety disorders, eating disorders, addictions, impulsive disorders, guilt problems, shame issues, panic disorders, and marital and relational struggles, find their root in conflicts with boundaries."[7]

Think of it this way: When people buy a home, they get what's called a plat. The plat lets the buyer know where the boundary lines are on their new property. It lets them know where their property ends and where their neighbor's property begins. The lines let the owners know what they're responsible for and what their neighbor is responsible for. The fact that you may be a negligent homeowner doesn't justify your neighbor cutting your grass, and vice versa! You are not responsible for your neighbor's property or her life. When one of you starts trying to take charge of the other's property, serious and unnecessary conflict will be inevitable.

With that in mind, let's talk about a few healthy boundaries you will need as you offer covering to your husband. The list is not comprehensive, but I hope you'll find it helpful. Let's begin.

Boundary No. 1: You're Responsible for You, I'm Responsible for Me

Ladies, I want to help set you free. It's not your responsibility to make an irresponsible man behave and live responsibly. If the man you're married to and committed to covering is irresponsible, that's his responsibility. You may be embarrassed by it, but it's not your responsibility. You should certainly pray for him, but don't make excuses for him. And be strong enough not to take responsibility for him.

You can't make him be on-time if he's chronically tardy. He'll have to endure the erosion of his reputation. It's his responsibility to rebuild it if he wants a good name. When he has embarrassed himself, it's not your job to make him feel better about it. "Oh, it's okay. You're a great guy. They didn't have to be so hard on you." Ladies, don't do that. Let him sit in the pain of his consequences. The Bible says, "If you rescue a man once, you'll have to do it again" (Proverbs 19:19). If he doesn't come to terms with his rashness or tardiness or whatever irresponsible ways he has, just let him deal with it. Complaining, moaning, and making it about you will not help. Just keep smiling and praying. But whatever you do, don't rescue him. You will further weaken his character and constitution as a man.

I've heard so many ladies say, "My husband won't get a job. I go to work every day. I'm trying to hold down the bills, but I can't get him motivated; I'm unable to inspire him to seize the opportunities before him." Seizing opportunities to support a household, going to work, paying the bills. It's all the same thing. If a man has a problem "beating the pavement" to find work … if he just won't go after what he needs to care of you and the home, you are in a tough position. Few things are more challenging than trying to light a fire under a man with no passion, no sense of urgency, and no drive to bring home at least some of the proverbial bacon.

I don't have an easy solution for what is usually a very complex issue. Kids and the costs of basic needs such as food, transportation, and housing are usually involved. Every situation is a little different. But I can tell you this: Your attempts to control his irresponsible life are not working out for either of you. One of the reasons many people are unhappy, negative, and breaking down is because they allow someone else's irresponsibility to drive them insane. But the immature person you may want to reign in is usually quite happy being immature and reckless (Proverbs 19:19).

I've learned the hard way that you cannot want more for people than they want for themselves. You cannot do for them what they're unwilling to do for themselves. Until the notion of progress and success costs them appropriately, they'll never ante up. No one who is unwilling to pay the price of success will ever value it. Even if you share your success with him, he won't know how to maintain it. Other people, even those you love deeply, will happily spend your resources for their own comfort and enjoyment. Unfortunately, until your man who refuses to grow up suffers the consequences for his unwise choices, you will be the only one bitter, frustrated, negative, and worry-filled.

When you take responsibility for yourself and let him take responsibility for himself, you're in line with Scripture. Galatians 6:5 is a tremendous help on this point: "For each one shall bear his own load." The word for load in the original language is *phortion*. You don't have to be a Greek scholar to get that. Everyone has to carry and be responsible for his or her own portion ... responsibility ... part ... task ... service. When you let him handle his portion—whatever you both agree to—both of you will be better off.

For the sake of clarity and for the record, a person's portion is different from his burden. Ladies, your man may be carrying his portion of the responsibilities. That's wonderful and that creates synergy and harmony in the home. But he may also be carrying a burden. A burden is heavy stuff that no one was meant to carry alone. In the family of God, we are commanded to carry one another's burdens. "Bear one another's burdens, and so fulfill the law of Christ" (Galatians 6:2). This is a love-your-neighbor kind of matter.

One of the ways you cover him is by helping him carry his burdens. And one of the ways he covers you is by helping you carry your burdens. The truth is, no one gets through life without having to bear burdens. Jesus said, "In this world you will have trouble. But take heart! I have overcome the world" (John 16:33b NIV). If we live, trouble is bound to come our way. We are going to face obstacles. We may face the devastating loss of loved ones and have to carry the burden of grief. We could suffer unanticipated, incapacitating illness that can radically change our lives and shatter our hopes and dreams. Unexpected layoffs that upend the family finances are very different from a refusal to seek employment. Those are burdens. And we are called to partner with one another in a way that is reciprocal: When one is burdened, the other helps carry some of the weight.

Sharing your husband's burden is a tremendous way to express your love and commitment to him. It's that *helper* thing in action. Some dear friends of ours were in the midst of extraordinary success in life while in their middle 40's. He was flourishing in his business career, and their family was enjoying the fruits of his labor. That's the way God intends—work hard, be rewarded, give God tithes and offerings of course, and enjoy the fruits of your hard work. Without warning signs or symptoms, he suffered a sudden aneurism while traveling for work in Brazil. That aneurism has left him unable to get back to his previous form as a high-capacity business executive. He struggles with his long-term memory and with walking stability.

To date, his wife is carrying the burden with him as his primary caretaker and motivator. There was a time when John could take great care of himself, his schedule, his travel, the finances, and his goals. Now, Greta helps him get dressed, schedules his medical care, and travels with him. He's still a huge Baltimore Ravens fan, so she makes sure he can get to the game with his buddies. The two of them seek God together, faithfully worshipping at church on Sundays. The adjustment to their lives, which includes their two college-aged daughters, has been anything but easy. But she is in a lane God has assigned her to as his wife. As challenging as her days have been the last six years, God has given her extraordinary grace and strength. Her husband's wellbeing is now her responsibility, and she has stepped into the role valiantly.

Boundary No. 2: I Can Say "Yes," or I Can Say "No"

The words *yes* and *no* are simple but powerful. They have extraordinary meaning for establishing boundary lines in all relationships. Yes is affirmative. It says in essence, "Cool. I'm good with the direction. Let's continue." No, on the other hand, is negative. It says, "Stop. I'm not in agreement. Let's not have that." I love how Matthew 5:37 is translated in the NIV: "All you need to say is simply 'Yes' or 'No'; anything beyond this comes from the evil one." Sisters, your yeses and your noes are the simplest and clearest ways to let your man (and anyone else, for that matter) know how you expect to be treated.

I'm less concerned with the verbal yes and the verbal no that you express in conversation. I'm more concerned, quite honestly, with your emotional yeses and noes—the ones you express to announce your boundary lines. These are the ones you shout from deep down on the inside of you and that you follow up on with clear actions. You see, ladies, you can say yes with your words but really deep inside feel a no in your heart. It's kind of like when my wife says to me, "I'm fine." But deep down inside she's not … and I know it. The same is true when your heart is saying no to the behavior of your man, but your actions are saying yes. Your inner answer—yes or no in your spirit—is the real answer. To keep the lines clear and to express your limits clearly, you have to go with the answer that's deep down on the inside.

> *When a woman says, "No," no matter the tone she uses, the man she's addressing had better acknowledge and respect the no. Ladies, your voice matters to God and it matters to respectable, honorable men.*

Can we take a brief interlude here? Let's leave no room for doubt. When a woman says, "No," no matter the tone she uses, the man she's addressing had better acknowledge and respect the *no*. Ladies, your voice matters to God and it matters to respectable, honorable men. But men who have violated women sexually and physically have no regard for women's *noes* or their voices. Too many of them have left women emotionally, spiritually, physically, and relationally wounded. I'm on a personal mission to address this perversion of masculinity that resides in so many men. And I'm committed to seeing women recover their voices.

For the sake of our discussion, my focus here is on relationship boundaries in the context of a marriage that may be struggling but is not abusive. These are the relationships in which women often struggle to be clear about their expectations of their men. Of course, you may not be married, but you may be in a close relationship with a man that you care for deeply. The same principles apply. If you're married to or in an intimate relationship with someone like I described above, please seek private counsel and support. Please text CONNECT to 741741 in the United States. No woman should have to live in a physically, verbally, sexually, or emotionally abusive relationship. You're worth way too much.

Shall we continue? Here's my strong admonition, ladies: Say yes or say no, but don't say both. Start with your inner response. Take a deep breath, pause, and listen to what you really feel and to what really matters to you on the issue. In most cases, this is not a moral contemplation. That is, there's no question of moral right or wrong involved. When a moral question is at issue, ask yourself why responding is creating a dilemma for you. Be honest and take the issue to God. You never have to do anything immoral or that violates your moral conscience in order to cover your man. And a good man who loves and cherishes you would never ask you to. You're even free to set some boundaries with a cheating or porn-addicted spouse. Here's why: "But now I am writing to you that you must not associate with anyone who claims to be a brother or sister but is sexually immoral or greedy, an idolater or slanderer, a drunkard or swindler. Do not even eat with such people" (1 Corinthians 5:11). At the end of the day, "We must obey God rather than human beings!" (Acts 5:29 NIV).

Once you've settled the issue, be courageous and make your verbal response line up with your inner response. Communicating yes when you really feel a no down inside only fosters instability in you. It robs you of your confidence and will cause resentment to grow in you. It may take years, but it will come out at some point, usually in inexplicable bursts of anger and bouts with depression. Constant accommodation without real conversation and truth-telling skews the boundaries. It opens a gateway for the enemy in your life and in your relationship. That's why Jesus says anything besides a clear and honest yes or no "comes from the evil one." A clear, firm, and consistent no is always much better than a soft yes.

Not everybody has this struggle with yesses and noes. Some people just say no to everyone, all the time, including the man they're wed to. That's called selfish, and it doesn't take long before it causes real problems in the relationship. "No, I don't feel like making love," day after day and night after night is problematic. You can't cover your husband when you're unwilling to share your body with him. "No, I'm busy. I can't get you a fresh shirt for your trip." Maybe you were busy, but could you find a gentler way to say no? How about, "I'd really love to do that for you. My meeting schedule is impossible today. You take the trip and I'll have my assistant ship three shirts overnight for you. Or, "I'll have them waiting for you when you get home." No can be clear and still have implied within it a very effective yes. But constant, uninterrupted noes construct a quick path to divorce court.

On the other hand, some people can't say no to anyone. That's called a lack of boundaries. That person doesn't know where she ends and others begin, what's her portion and what's not. If you've suffered abuse, neglect, or abandonment, you may have trouble with this. We all fear anger, disappointment, lost love, lack of approval, and loss of relationship to some degree. But honestly, we've come to value what people think of us way too much! And that clouds our judgment. Many people are so addicted to approval that they misjudge the approval they may already have in the eyes of the person who covers them. So we say yes, but it's really out of compulsion (2 Corinthians 9:7).

You may struggle with duplicity (i.e., feeling an inner no but communicating an outer *yes*) because you feel a need to please your man. You may not want to disappoint him, or you may fear losing your connection to him. Remember, one of the key reasons for being clear is to tell people how you expect to be treated. If you continue to be duplicitous, you'll lose closeness with him anyway because of your resentment and/or his failure to feed your legitimate emotional needs. It's a sure recipe for problems.

So often women will allow a man to neglect them emotionally, live financially irresponsibly, or even ignore their physical needs. It usually happens when a woman's real no is communicated as a yes. A young woman came to me recently who was in a long-term "committed" relationship with a man in his early thirties. She has a stable job with good benefits and reasonable pay and has been working diligently to save and prepare for purchasing a home. A home will provide her (and him) with a degree of housing stability and potential generational wealth if stewarded properly. She really wants to be married. He's not interested. In fact, he doesn't even have a job! She works long, demanding days, while he sleeps late and explains, "Nobody's hiring."

When she came to me, the first measure of relief for me as her pastor was that they don't have any children together. This young woman has made some costly mistakes, largely because she never had the covering of her father. She has allowed the lines, lanes, and limits to get very fuzzy and convoluted. She's trying to cover someone who is not committed to covering her as a husband. When I asked her why she allows him to live in her apartment like an irresponsible bum, she said, "He makes me feel guilty." "He tells me that I don't love him because I put pressure on him and threaten to put him out." Okay, at this point out comes my not-so-pastoral side. "Who gives a d---! Get that bum out of your house and get on with your life! You don't need his help to do badly. You seem perfectly capable of doing badly enough all by yourself."

Now for my more pastoral side. (Help me, Holy Spirit.) She wants better, and she really wants to move on with her life without him. But she keeps communicating yes when she really is feeling no. She just hasn't found the courage to be consistent because she has become a people-pleaser who is easily manipulated emotionally. I've started teaching on value and healthy relationships recently, and she has begun to align her inner no with her outer no.

Ladies, you may love that man, but you can learn to establish healthy limits around your life. Yes, you can. You can put a stop to the people-pleasing and being manipulated. You can be clear about your boundaries. You don't have to say yes when you really mean no. Your choices belong to you. Stop giving people unlimited access to your emotions—room to abuse your goodness. Even the man you are called to cover as your husband will be better off if you're clear about your boundaries. He'll get a more confident, more beautiful you.

Boundary No. 3: You Can't Handle Me Like You Handle Them

> *"Husbands, in the same way be considerate as you live with your wives, and treat them with respect as the weaker partner and as heirs with you of the gracious gift of life, so that nothing will hinder your prayers."* (1 Peter 3:7)

An NFL locker room is a unique environment. Most women have never been inside of one before practice, after practice, or on game day. Ladies, it's hard for me to convey to you what it's like. But I loved it when I was the chaplain of the Baltimore Ravens from 1999 to 2012. It was a bastion of male humor, male camaraderie, roughhousing, cornhole competitions, and a few other things that absolutely need the redemption of Jesus. I was right at home in the locker room because I'm a guy, and I get guy humor. I'm competitive. I also know the pains and frustrations guys hide in the locker room's sea of testosterone and masculinity.

Honestly ladies, there's no need for you to be familiar with what goes on in an NFL players' locker room. Men still need some spaces that are sacred. The challenge is that sometimes players take the locker room home with them. Often, in my ministry as a chaplain and life coach to couples in the NFL, wives complained about one thing consistently: "He talks to me as if I'm one of the guys." Rarely did I hear that complaint without tears. The men were so accustomed to their world in the locker room that they forgot something very important. Most people, especially their wives, were not built for the rough, gruff, raw language and humor they were accustomed to spouting at work.

The principle is this: Men are men and women are women. I had to remind the players not to take the locker room home because their wives were not NFL athletes! I had to train players to code switch—i.e., to learn to separate and use languages and behaviors appropriate to the environments they were in. Home is not an NFL locker room!

One of the critical boundaries you must draw with your man, ladies, is this one: "You cannot handle me like you handle them." Just because cussing and brash language are allowed in most male-dominated environments doesn't mean you should be subjected to it at home with your husband. Just because guys can dole out harsh jokes with each other and rip each other to shreds with words that might devastate the average person doesn't mean you should allow him to bring that kind of roasting humor home to you. You have to draw a really thick and clear line. You have to demand to be treated on the basis of three things: *consideration*, *respect*, and *prayer*.

Remind the man you cover as his Eve that you expect consideration. The NIV uses the phrase "be considerate." The NKJV says, "dwell with them with understanding." The idea is that your husband must live with you with a deeper understanding of who you are, what matters to you, what has hurt you in the past, and what would hurt you today. He's got to pause for the cause when he's dealing with you, so that he's careful not to crush you with harsh words, rough touches, brutal humor. You're not his male counterpart. You're his other half, the partner who makes his life complete. He can't be his best if you're not your best. And you can't be your best if he's not treating you with his absolute best. He must take all of you—your journey, your wounds, your temperament, your feelings, and your destiny—into consideration when he's handling you.

The apostle Peter sets down the rule when he writes, "Husbands, likewise, dwell with them with understanding, giving honor to the wife, as to the weaker vessel, and as being heirs together of the grace of life, that your prayers may not be hindered" (1 Peter 3:7). The word for "honor" in this passage is translated from the Greek word *time* (tee-may). I love the idea behind this word. It speaks of the value of something, money paid for something. It suggests that something is precious and that it should be esteemed to the highest degree because it has extraordinary, inherent value. And just so we're clear, there are still some things money can't buy or give worth to. I tell people all the time, "Your job can never pay you what you're worth because your worth is not tied to your employment." People can pay for your work, but they can't pay for your worth.

In your love relationship with the man you cover, remind him that you're worth so much, he could spend the next 100 years buying you things and never scratch the surface of your value. Because God places such value and honor on your life, don't ever settle for dishonor. Don't ever settle for words toward you or about you that pull you down to a dog's level. That man of yours will compromise his covering and make himself open to God's judgment if he dishonors you that way. Love him enough to let him know that the blessing of God upon is life is contingent upon his honoring you.

The blessing upon his life is also connected to whether he can get a prayer through to God. If he insists on bringing the locker room home, he will shut up heaven's favor toward his life. I'm totally convinced that many men have lost NFL and other lucrative careers because they disregarded this principle. God is clear that a man who is inconsiderate of his wife and treats her with dishonor is standing under a closed heaven. No favor. No open doors. No promotion. No divine opportunities. In fact, God says their prayers will be cut down and frustrated. Since your job is to cover him and his job is to cover you, remind him when he dishonors you that God has just hit the switch to close up the floodgates of heaven's blessing toward him. Not until he repents and makes it right will access to God and answers to prayer become available again.

Chapter 10 Reflections:

1. Many men will not respect a woman who allows herself to be treated any kind of way by her man or by anyone else. So when you value and regard yourself with clear boundaries, men know you're not to be taken lightly. Real men respect that.

2. Husbands and wives are called to cover each other, but we're not responsible for each other's reactions, behaviors, and responsibilities. You will become stifled and anxiety-filled if you try to live according to other peoples' unfair and unrealistic expectations of you.

3. When a woman says, "No," no matter the tone she uses, the man she's addressing had better acknowledge and respect the *no*. Ladies, your voice matters to God and it matters to respectable, honorable men.

4. You can put a stop to the people-pleasing and being manipulated. You can be clear about your boundaries. You don't have to say yes when you really mean no. Your choices belong to you. Stop giving people unlimited access to your emotions—room to abuse your goodness.

11

Embrace Wild With Him
Adventure And Exploration
(Joshua 14:6-15)

The likelihood is that your man is not interested in "going where no man has ever gone before." He might be the rare guy with a goal to summit Mt. Kilimanjaro, K2, or Everest, but not likely. That certainly isn't my thing. I would wager, however, (if I were a betting man) that he still has his expression of a wild side. There's a part of all men—no matter how small it is or how dormant it lies—that likes to explore, to discover, to "check it out," to try something new, to take a risk, to get that exhilarating rush that comes with jumping off the high-dive for the first time! When that part of a man is gone, he's no fun and he probably should consider getting some counseling.

When we were kids, my older brother liked to pretend he was the famed stunt man, Evel Knievel. Like his daredevil, hero, he built ramps to make his bike soar in the sky. Of course, he only jumped four or five feet, but the adventure was a success for an eight-year-old little boy. I recall making go-carts out of grocery carts. Somehow, we would detach the large basket part from the frame and wheels on the bottom portion. In those days, there were no bicycle helmet laws. I'm not even sure we owned bicycle helmets. By the amazing grace of God, I'm still alive, even after a downhill run with no brakes. I have no idea what I was thinking or how the makeshift go-cart came to a stop. I didn't care. I was all in for the adventure. My wild side had kicked in!

After I was older but still young enough to go for it, I drove our new minivan from Maryland to LA in three days, alone – with a paper map. There was no GPS. When I made it to Albuquerque, New Mexico, all the hotels were sold out. No problem. I spent the night on the back seat. Did I mention the temperature dipped to 40 degrees? It was all good. I was excited about a new ministry assignment in LA. I didn't care how I got there or that there were no more hotel rooms. A new journey was awaiting me. (Sheri and our firstborn were waiting for me too; I'd flown them out ahead of me.) It was all about exploring, seeing some new places, embracing a challenge.

Travel, new cities, new countries, new food, and nowadays a nice car (preferably one with some throat and some horsepower) let me express my wild side. For some guys it means flying down the highway at 100-plus miles an hour on the motorcycle of their childhood dreams. For others of us it means camping out in the Grand Canyon for days or weeks. For some guys it means cross-country trips in RVs and fly-fishing on remote lakes in the mountains known for their trophy wild trout. And for others it's starting, acquiring, scaling, or selling another business. It's all about rush, risk, and reward!

> *If you attempt to tame your man, one of two things will happen. First, he may give in and become a soft guy with questionable fortitude. He will lose his moxie, his grit, his will to lead. You'll be stuck with a guy who is always unsure of himself and who will take little initiative when it's most needed. Or second, you will end up with a man who deeply resents you.*

I don't know what it is for your man, but the appetite to discover, to explore, to venture out, and to conquer can be insatiable. May we never get over it! Writer John Eldredge touched a nerve in millions of men when he wrote and released his first book, *Wild at Heart*, in 2001. It's like men were starving for someone to put into writing "that thing" in us that women were not quite getting. That thing in us is our wild side. Unfortunately, many men have allowed their wild side to be tamed or have let their wild side lead them into sin, folly, and destruction.

The latter is not what I'm talking about. By wild, I don't mean plunging into things that are immoral, damaging to the soul, or dishonoring to God. Wild is not code for foolish and sinful. But nothing makes the adventure more enjoyable than to have a woman in our lives who doesn't merely tolerate our wild side, but who also celebrates it. Few things scream, "I deeply respect you!" louder than a woman who gets into a man's adventures with him. Ladies, if you're going to cover your man well, you cannot resist his wild side. You don't have to understand it. You don't even have to like it. But you will have to give him room to do something other than go to work, come home for dinner, and pay the bills. Below are some ways you can encourage and embrace your man's wild side.

Dream About It with Him

You're in a great position to help your man get his dream life back if he's lost it. Dream with him. Just ask him, "What would you do just for you, if you could take the time out of your schedule and money was not an obstacle?" Those are the two things that stifle a man's dreams—time and money. Deficits of time and money make men obsessed with responsibilities. That's not a bad thing unless he has stopped dreaming and has no outlets for adventure. Like someone said, "All work and no play makes _____ a dull boy."

From the time I was in high school, I had a passion for photography. My mom heard about it and bought me my first 35mm camera—a Pentax K1000. It was awesome! I loved that camera because it helped me express my passion for art, my enjoyment of nature, and my love for my family. I took thousands of pictures of my kids with that camera when I was a new dad. And I took it on every trip around the country with me. The pictures were so-so, but the photo adventures to the South Rim of the Grand Canyon, the Poudre Canyon in Colorado, and Big Bear Lake in California are unforgettable. We still have a lot of those photos in old-fashioned scrapbooks, and my adult kids love looking at them.

The shutterbug in me is still very much alive. It's how I zone out from the rigors of ministry to people. Sheri is my biggest fan. She recently asked me the question I posed to you. I said I'd like to go take a travel photo course for my favorite genre—landscape photography. I have a dream of opening an art gallery that features my work and that of other artists. Thanks to Sheri's support of my wild side, I get to go away for hours and for days to cool places, climbing rocks, taking desolate roads, and walking trails, to take photographs. My equipment has improved significantly over the years and so have my eye and technique. I couldn't imagine the hole I'd be trying to fill in my life if Sheri hadn't continued to champion my photography itch. Of course, she also loves that her home gets peppered with beautiful, gallery-quality art for free.

Help Him Pack for It

Do you want to breathe life into his wild side? Then pull out the suitcase. Run down to the local Target or REI and stock up on all the things he'll need. Will he need batteries, new toiletries, wool socks, a new camping grill, mosquito repellent? I have no idea what he needs. You may not know either, but ask him for a list well in advance of his next adventure.

Trust me, when you come home with the car loaded from his shopping list, he'll turn into a twelve-year-old boy—in the best ways, of course. He'll be thinking about you the entire trip away, girlfriend! He may be off expressing his wild side, but he may never feel closer to you. That special shopping trip, your endorsement of his wild side, and every item he holds in his hand will remind him who is for him. You. I know it's not a competition, but I can all but guarantee that if he's adventuring with a group of guys, none of their wives shopped for them and packed for them the way you will have. You will be the bomb-diggity!

Don't Try to Tame Him

Real men can't be totally tamed. That's my opinion and I'm sticking to it! If you attempt to tame your man, one of two things will happen. First, he may give in and become a soft guy with questionable fortitude. He will lose his moxie, his grit, his will to lead. You'll be stuck with a guy who is always unsure of himself and who will take little initiative when it's most needed. Or second, you will end up with a man who deeply resents you. He may go to work, come home for dinner, and make sure responsibilities are taken care of. But he will have a difficult time drawing close to you emotionally and abandoning himself fully to you. If you tame him, you take away his male grit! Don't do it to him. And since I'm on this point … don't do it to your sons either! If they marry, their wives will come to resent you too and perhaps rue the day they married your baby boy.

As we noted in a previous chapter, Michal, King David's wife, made an emotionally fatal mistake with him because she tried to bridle his wild passion for God. I love David. He was a man's man—a man of passion, a man who made man-mistakes, a man who would go toe-to-toe with God's enemies no matter their size. He took out the nine-foot giant named Goliath with one out of five smooth stones—hit him right between the eyes, and the battle was over. I love that he went over to him and cut off his head and took his sword. That's what you have to do as a man. You gotta cut down any enemy that comes against your destiny, threatens your house, and talks trash. You gotta cut off his head to make sure he's dead and take his sword so the world will know that you're God's man and you are serious about it. Don't judge me. I'm not violent. I'm just wild for God! And my Bible tells me this was God's sentiment toward him: "I have found David the son of Jesse, a man after My own heart, who will do all My will" (Acts 13:22). Why would anyone try to tame a man like that?

David was finally able to bring the ark of God into the city of David, Jerusalem, the nation's newly established capital. It was a day of dancing and celebration, and the new king danced wildly before the LORD. I can only imagine the passion and the joy and all the emotional exuberance. You have to get the picture in your mind of this valiant man losing all inhibitions, twirling in the streets with the people. God, who is David's passion, has also been his protection in the wilderness after thirteen years of running from King Saul. He can't help but dance; he's got a lot of reasons to praise God. I want to dance right now, just thinking about that magnificent day of ushering in God's presence so the house of Israel could be blessed (see 2 Samuel 6:12-23).

Michal, David's reward wife for killing Goliath and Saul's daughter, couldn't stand to see the wild warrior-turned-king act so undignified in the presence of the commoners. Boy, did she miss her moment! Watching from an upstairs window in the palace, "she despised David in her heart" (2 Samuel 6:16b). Her first problem was that she didn't get that her place was at the king's side. She should've been wildly dancing right next to David. Instead, she hated the fact that he'd disrobed and displayed all of his wild side in public. In short, she hated that she couldn't tame him. When he come in the door of the palace, she gave the king all of her mind—all of it.

As I said, it was an emotionally fatal move. She tried to tame a wild man. She tried to put him in his place. But David was no punk king. He was a man's man who walked in the authority of God and who loved the people. David would not be controlled and domesticated. That day spelled the end for Michal. She never saw the king again. He never touched her intimately. Imagine the regret she lived with. Imagine what could have been hers had she celebrated the beautiful, God-honoring wildness of her man. She could have been the woman rubbing the king's back. He might never have slept with Bathsheba. He would perhaps have felt no need. Her son might have become Israel's next king instead of Solomon. Who knows?

So what are you saying, Rod? I'm simply saying, because you're called to cover your man, not to control him, it's better you celebrate his wild side with him. Come down from your high place, if you have one, and join him for a wild ride, emotionally and physically, when necessary. God gave you to him so you could be his closest, wildest friend in life.

Chapter 11 Reflections:

1. You're in a great position to help your man get his dream life back if he's lost it. Dream with him. Just ask him, "What would you do just for you, if you could take the time out of your schedule and money was not an obstacle?"

2. If you attempt to tame your man, one of two things will happen. First, he may give in and become a soft guy with questionable fortitude. He will lose his moxie, his grit, his will to lead. You'll be stuck with a guy who is always unsure of himself and who will take little initiative when it's most needed. Or second, you will end up with a man who deeply resents you.

12

Get *Him*
No One Should Know Him Like You Do

On one level, men are very simple. A little food, a little sex, a good job, and a little sleep go a long way for a man. On another level, we can be very complex individuals. We can be moody. Some days we're charging great hills in life, confidently taking hold of our destiny. On another day, we're uncertain of our direction and wondering if we're doing the right thing at the right time. Some days we're overwhelmed by the big picture of our responsibilities, and on other days we're struggling to find balance because we just can't get enough of our work. We can have all of that going on while we're tossing balls to our sons and playing dolls with our daughters.

While many women stereotype men with simple labels, exclaiming the unfortunate generality, "All men are the same!", men are shouting back, "It's absolutely untrue!" The truth is, no two men are alike. Not all men enjoy eighteen holes of golf. For some men like me, eighteen holes of golf feels like a punishment for bad behavior in class. My ADHD can't handle it. Not all men like fast cars. (I can't imagine why not! That baffles me.) Not all men care who's playing in the MLB (baseball), NBA (basketball), or NFL (football) championships. Some guys love sports while other guys loathe sports. We're as varied as the colors of flowers in your garden.

But one thing we do have in common when it come to our women is this: We want you to get us. If you're going to honor your assignment to cover us, we really need you to get us. If you want to know how to bring out the best in your man, you gotta learn to get *him*. Because even men long to be deeply known by somebody—not everybody, but at least by the one we've tied our lives to in matrimony.

Ladies, have you studied your man's idiosyncrasies? Do you know when his cup is empty? Can you tell when he needs rest? Have you figured out his rhythms and when he's going to need some time alone? Is his favorite meal in the Notes app on your iPhone? Does his brain need time to wake up in the morning or is he a talker early in the day? How often does he need sexual intimacy (assuming he's your marriage partner)? What breaks his heart? What thrills his spirit? Who absolutely gets under his skin? How does he wear stress? What are his fears?

I could go on and on, but I don't want your relationship with your man to become a research project. It should, however, become a matter of prayer, observation, wisdom, and strategy. Remember, there's gold buried in the heart and soul of your man, and you should be on a mission to mine it because the world needs what's inside of him. That's why "A word fitly spoken is like apples of gold / In settings of silver" (Proverbs 25:11). And, "Counsel in the heart of man is like deep water, / But a [woman] of understanding will draw it out" (Proverbs 20:5).

According to the writer of Proverbs, there is *counsel* deep inside a man's gut. In the Bible the heart was considered the center of human life. Today we say, "What are you sensing in your *gut*?" It's the same idea. The counsel in the heart or gut of a man refers to advisement, prudence, or purpose. It's really what's in his mind. It's what he's thinking and considering. It's the questions he's asking: "What's next? ... Should I? ... When is the best time to make the move? ... How should I handle the situation I'm dealing with?" A woman of understanding is able to help him process counsel and come up with God's best for the two of them. That's a tall order, which can only be scaled with wisdom, insight, and prayer by the woman who studies her man and gets *him*.

What's on a man's mind—that is, the counsel in his heart—has to be *drawn* out. Ladies, you can't nag it out of him. You can't badger him about it. Well, you could, but getting it out using those methods won't draw him closer to you. It'll make him want to be anywhere other than where you are. Those methods create way too much unwanted pressure for us. The counsel of our hearts must be drawn out gently and steadily, like drawing water from a well. That's the picture created by the word *out* in Proverbs 20:5. It's that of using a bucket to draw water out of a well. I've had that farming experience as a kid. And the lessons I remember are these: (1) There's nothing cooler and more refreshing than well water fed from an underground spring! (2) If you pull up your bucket too hard and too fast, you lose half the water by the time the bucket reaches you. (3) And the deeper the well, the more time it takes. If you're skilled at drawing out the counsel, you'll get all of it … at the right time!

And just for the record, getting *him* is not a one-way street. He must also learn to get you. If you will allow me to adapt a principle from Scripture, he should "study [you] to show himself approved" (see 2 Timothy 2:15). That includes the word and his woman. As your husband, he must live with you with understanding and show you honor (1 Peter 3:7). That means God does not give him permission to dismiss you when he doesn't understand you. Nor does he get to belittle you when your idiosyncrasies leave him stumped.

> *One of the biggest disappointments men express to me is, "She just doesn't get me." Many men feel lonely, unknown, and largely unconsidered when it comes to all the elements of their lives that contribute to who they are. The fact that it's difficult for men to put those things into words does not negate the fact that all men want to be safely and confidentially known.*

Sisters, as you work to *get him*, give yourself lots of grace and room for growth. Your journey is neither for novice wives nor for the weak at heart. Ask God for wisdom and insight into his heart and his needs. Ask your man what he would like you to understand better about him. In fact, ask him to share five important things that he needs from you. And keep in mind that what he needed at twenty-seven is very different from what he will need at forty-seven, fifty-seven, or seventy-five. Because most women desire to be pleasing to the men in their lives, there will be the temptation to stress, to try too hard, or to give up. Do your best to avoid all of those extremes.

Trust that because God has assigned you to the man in your life, He will give you the knowledge and the understanding you need in order to bring out the best in him. "For the Lord gives wisdom; / From His mouth come knowledge and understanding" (Proverbs 2:6). On your journey to *getting him* you might want to keep a private notebook, because revelation insights are about to flow—possibly faster than your brain can organize them. Even as you read the rest of this chapter and wind down the book, things about your man will come to your mind. But this time you'll find yourself connecting dots. Look for times to talk with him, ask him questions, and listen to his heart. Remember, that's where all his counsel is. One question a day might be all he or his life will have room for. Just pull up your bucket slowly with each filling of counsel.

This chapter of *Cover Him* is potentially the most important one. One of the biggest disappointments men express to me is, "She just doesn't get me." Many men feel lonely, unknown, and largely unconsidered when it comes to all the elements of their lives that contribute to who they are. The fact that it's difficult for men to put those things into words does not negate the fact that all men want to be safely and confidentially known. The men who feel *un-gotten* and *unknown are particularly susceptible to affairs, pornography addictions, drug and alcohol addictions, and depression.* So ladies, don't skip this chapter. In fact, slow down and give it your full attention. Your man is waiting for you to fully get him.

Get His Story

All our lives are one big story. We're born into a family somewhere on the globe. We grow up in some community or several of them. Trauma and drama happen to most of us along the way and impact how we see life, others, and ourselves. Our experiences shape our stories, influencing our choices. We choose colleges or careers or neither. At some point people usually give love a try, which means other people bring their stories to our life stories. Our adult years are spent surviving, thriving, and sometimes avoiding the costs associated with life.

After a while we become acquainted with loss and grief, which also impact our stories. Relationships come and relationships go; some mean more than others. And to the degree that we are connected to people (or should have been connected to them) they color our stories. For many of my readers, their stories were interrupted by an amazing lover whose name is Jesus. Through Him so many of us have found new beginnings in our stories. Faith. Forgiveness. The ability to forgive others who've hurt us. Our stories have taken a drastic turn away from who we had become in many aspects, to who we were created to be. God's huge story of creation, fall, and redemption is impacting people's stories all over the world. I'm one who has been thusly impacted, and I can't tell my story without telling that story.

Ladies, your man has a story. No matter what it is, no matter how much he loathes it or likes it, it's powerful. It means something and it matters. It's his story, and no matter how many painful chapters there may be to it, his is not a haphazard story. He's here on purpose, and the Story Maker has been guarding His divine pen very carefully.

You don't have to do a deep-dive study on this text right now, but you really should do it sometime. Look at what David wrote in Psalm 139:1-18:

O Lord, You have searched me and known me.
You know my sitting down and my rising up;
You understand my thought afar off.
You comprehend my path and my lying down,
And are acquainted with all my ways.
For there is not a word on my tongue,
But behold, O Lord, You know it altogether.
You have hedged me behind and before,
And laid Your hand upon me.
Such knowledge is too wonderful for me;
It is high, I cannot attain it.
Where can I go from Your Spirit?
Or where can I flee from Your presence?
If I ascend into heaven, You are there;
If I make my bed in hell, behold, You are there.
If I take the wings of the morning,
And dwell in the uttermost parts of the sea,
Even there Your hand shall lead me,
And Your right hand shall hold me.
If I say, "Surely the darkness shall fall on me,"
Even the night shall be light about me;
Indeed, the darkness shall not hide from You,
But the night shines as the day;
The darkness and the light are both alike to You.
For You formed my inward parts;

You covered me in my mother's womb.
I will praise You, for I am fearfully and wonderfully made;
Marvelous are Your works,
And that my soul knows very well.
My frame was not hidden from You,
When I was made in secret,
And skillfully wrought in the lowest parts of the earth.
Your eyes saw my substance, being yet unformed.
And in Your book they all were written,
The days fashioned for me,
When as yet there were none of them.
How precious also are Your thoughts to me, O God!
How great is the sum of them!
If I should count them, they would be more in number than the sand;
When I awake, I am still with You.

Forgive my partiality, but every time I read this section of Psalm 139, I feel that David wrote this for me. But really, God led David to write a summary of his own story to encourage every person's story who has a relationship with God. Even if you or your man don't have a relationship with God, David's story is the reminder that each of our stories has been carefully written by an amazing God. He's been there all along, and he's fully aware of every detail of your story and your husband's story.

He knew what each of our days would hold before any of them ever rolled around on the calendar. He knew the good days and the bad days that would come into our stories. He knew the sunny days and the very dark days that "try the souls of men"—what the sixteenth-century mystic writer and poet St. John of the Cross calls the "dark night of the soul." Of course, you know that your man has had some good days and some weary days with some hills to climb. But have you gotten to know his story well enough that you can tell it like a good historian—weaving in and out of the parts that are most relevant to your audience?

When you get that good at telling his story, you're on your way to getting him. When you can talk about the joys and challenges surrounding his birth, you're getting him. When you know that his mother struggled too much to keep him and gave him to his grandmother or that he was the joy of her life, you're getting into his water bucket. What part did his dad play in his early years, especially that crucial stage at age nine, where most kids' roles on the playground give a clear indication of their vocational roles in life? Was your man a leader picking the teams or was he on the sideline waiting to be chosen to play? Or was he still in the classroom working on something more interesting to him?

Who were his childhood friends? What was his biggest childhood pain or disappointment? Who believed in him and breathed the breath of life into him along the way? Did his parents love each other, or did they simply tolerate each other? Was home a place of joy or was it like a prison that one longs to escape? What role did faith play in his story? Does he believe that the Story Maker really loves him? When and why did he come to his particular conclusion about the Story Maker?

You'll have to come up with some of your own questions, but I think you can see that every man's answers to those kinds of questions are unique to him. That's because everyone has a unique story. To make yourself the queen of covering your man, gently lower your bucket into his well and bring up some water. If he only gives you a partial filling, thank God for the drink, even if it wasn't very tasty, and add it to your Notes app. The more you get, the more you will get him.

Get What Hurt Him

Every man's story has pain points in it. Hard times, disappointments, failures, broken hearts, and broken dreams make us who we are far more than success does. Success is great, but it tends to hide who we are. As you start delving into your man's story, sit quietly for the sentences laden with heartaches, grief, loss, abandonment, abuse, and betrayal.

You can't really know what moves and motivates a man until you know what has hurt a man. David lamented deeply in Psalm 55:12-15 the wounds caused by a close friend. It's as if he never fully got over it:

> For it is not an enemy who taunts me—
> then I could bear it;
> it is not an adversary who deals insolently with me—

then I could hide from him.
But it is you, a man, my equal,
my companion, my familiar friend.
We used to take sweet counsel together;
within God's house we walked in the throng.
Let death steal over them;
let them go down to Sheol alive;
for evil is in their dwelling place and in their heart.

You know who wounded your husband, but do you know what hurt him the most about it? Were they close friends? Family? Neighbors? Did they serve in church together? What exactly happened in their relationship? David prayed that death would stealthily come upon his old friend. That's a hurt man, right there. And in this psalm his memory is fresh as if the hurt happened that very day. That's how old wounds can be. They can bleed years later just as if the wound were fresh if we don't move purposefully toward healing.

Who were your man's previous close friends? What happened to the relationships? And how has he worked through the pain? Answers to those questions may help you understand why he keeps to himself or keeps potential friends at arm's length. Maybe his hurts have turned him into a champion of compassion for people who've been mistreated or a champion of reconciliation. Is he the guy who just wants everybody to get along? His hurts are a valuable clue to what motivates him in life. Because of my own father-wounds, I've focused a good deal of my energy on men and marriages. My passion has evolved out of my pain, and I really hope you're blessed by that.

Get What Dream Is in Him

A final big piece to the puzzle of getting your man is the dream that's way down on the inside of him. Sometimes the dream is not necessarily his wild side. It can be a vision to build an organization, a non-profit, buy a home in a particular city or setting, send his kids or other kids to college. I can't stress enough how important it is that you stimulate or reawaken the dreams in your man as one of the ways you cover him. A man who stops dreaming is dying. It won't be long before he gives up on life and settles for a rocker, the TV, and a twelve-pack of Budweiser every night.

I watched it happen to my good friend's dad when I was growing up. I was too young to know what I was watching unfold before my eyes then. But I think I know now. His dreams dried up in him. Every day after work, he came home, played with the dog, and cleaned up the poop. He drove a really cool, all-white Chrysler Cordoba with red accents and wood trim. I was fond of him because my dad was not in my life. But the puzzle began to come together after some time. He was that guy who drank two six-packs of Busch beer every night as he lay across the bed watching TV. He had no excitement in his life as I recall … except for the woman across town. My buddy and I spotted him going in and out of a woman's home where his car was parked outside. Maybe it wasn't what we thought, but we wouldn't bet our money on it to this day. And yes, my friend confronted his dad, and he denied it completely.

He was still a great guy. No judgment. But I really suspect that his dreams died. I don't know what they were, but he'd fully settled into a ho-hum routine. I wonder if he hadn't replaced his unfulfilled dreams with Busch beer, routine, meticulous manicuring of this 20x30-foot fenced lawn, and the mysterious lady across town.

If you do nothing else to cover your man, listen to his dreams. Fuel his dreams with articles, tickets to events that remind him, and constant affirmations that say, "I can see you doing that someday." Ask him to create a timeline with daily, monthly, and annual steps toward his dream. Celebrate the big steps with him. But whatever you do, never tell him it's impossible. Read his plan and reread it until it's as clear to you as it is to him. When you talk about the dream together, use *we* language like this: "When we …". When you start doing that, he'll know that you not only get his dream, but you get him.

Nothing will take your man higher in life than being able to say confidently, "Oh yeah. My wife really does get me. She knows all my quirks, and she is cool with me. No one has ever been more in my corner." Congratulations to you, my sister! You officially get him, and you're definitely covering him.

Chapter 12 Reflections:

1. If you're going to honor your assignment to cover us, we really need you to get us. If you want to know how to bring out the best in your man, you gotta learn to get *him*. Because even men long to be deeply known by somebody.

2. One of the biggest disappointments men express to me is, "She just doesn't get me." Many men feel lonely, unknown, and largely unconsidered when it comes to all the elements of their lives that contribute to who they are. The fact that it's difficult for men to put those things into words does not negate the fact that all men want to be safely and confidentially known.

3. Nothing will take your man higher in life than being able to say confidently, "Oh yeah. My wife really does get me. She knows all my quirks, and she is cool with me. No one has ever been more in my corner." Congratulations to you, my sister! You officially get him, and you're definitely covering him.

13

Give Him Some Rooms
He Needs Personal Space
And A Personal Place

I have no idea who came up with the idea of a "man cave"—a room in the house that a man can call his own, where he can slip away to be alone, watch a movie, play a game of pool, or take a nap. If it was a woman, I want to give her a big fat kiss on the forehead and present her with an award. If it was a guy, I want to give him a big "bro-hug" and a high-five. What a brilliant concept!

Men need room. And if I may, men need more than one room. We need *rooms*. I'm speaking metaphorically here. We need several places and spaces in order for us to be and become our best. Think of a room as a place of margin or a place of separation for focus on particular aspects of his life. Ladies, the man in your life could be screaming on the inside for some separate space for his soul.

A man without *rooms* is a man waiting to explode … or explode again. If the entire house is dedicated to the kids, the furniture, your projects, and who knows what else, your man is a forgotten entity. He needs space of his own. God designed men so that we compartmentalize our existence. In other words, if I'm working, I'm working. That's not the time when I like to talk. If I'm watching the game, that's the time that I can escape the demands of life for a couple of hours. Please don't bring me the bills while I'm watching the game. If I'm fighting a war, I set my emotions aside for the sake of duty. We live with compartments.

As men, we compartmentalize in the sense that we process our thoughts and prioritize information differently than women, overall. It's part of the way God has wired our brains. Says, Mike Yarbrough of Wolf & Iron, "Men typically have greater concentrations of neural pathways between the front and rear areas of the brain. The back of the brain is dominant in perception while the front is dominant in action."[8] Men are wired for action more than for emotional perusal and reflection. If there's a problem, our mental path leads to finding a solution—not to our (or your) feelings.

Like anything else that is normal or usual, "too far east is west." A good thing can become a bad thing. Too much strength in one direction becomes a weakness. Compartmentalizing too much for too long can lead to a disconnect from reality or to life imbalance. We reserve discussion about certain areas of life for particular places and environments, i.e., work at the office, faith at church, mistresses for travel, and football at the stadium. But such excessive

Ladies, you can give your man room to be real if you will not be shocked by anything he tells you. Can you handle his honesty about your weaknesses? Can he tell you when he feels you are not attending to him without you becoming defensive?

compartmentalization hinders our ability to live nuanced, holistic, and integrity-filled lives.

But for the sake of our discussion, let's assume we have achieved balance, health, and perspective in our various areas of life. When this is the case, compartmentalizing has great benefits. It's what enables men to stick to long, arduous, demanding tasks. It's what enables us to think like a football coach under pressure to score in the last two minutes of the game. Some people call it a one-track mind or being in the zone. And the more we do it, the more we're able to do it—for good or for bad.

But if you notice the man you love always running off to one of his *rooms* while you have to handle the rest of life in his absence, that's a problem. We're not naturally multitaskers like you women are, but we can certainly learn how to multitask and how to integrate, i.e., feelings and instructions. If *rooms* are a way of escape all the time, that's a weakness. And if those rooms include stashes of addictive substances like video games, marijuana, pornography, or alcohol, seek out a credible and effective counselor who specializes in a biblical understanding of manhood and womanhood. But the need is still the same. Men need room. In fact, men need several rooms.

Room to Think

I'm not very good with my hands. I wish I were, but I'm not. I used to think I was. I've done a few woodworking projects, tiled the kitchen backsplash, and painted the house many times. But truthfully, I'm not very handy. I work better with my mind. And looking back, I can see that I was always the geeky, cerebral type growing up.

Because of that, I need room to think—space in my day and a place in the house where I can sit quietly and think. When I'm having *think time*, I think about all sorts of things—how to move the church forward, what Sheri needs, the best direction to take over the next one, three, or five years. I think about books I'd like to write, people I need to connect with, and ideas I'd like to flesh out.

I'm a thinker by nature. But I think all men want room to think. We are given to solving problems, and problem-solving requires thinking. So ladies, if you really want to cover your man, give him some room to think when he needs it. Some people can handle constant noise, but noise interrupts the thinking process. That's why men will often say to screaming kids while driving down the highway, "Shut up! I'm trying to think."

He may not need a special room for thinking, ladies. But he will need you to give him room to think. If you can get ahead of this and figure out when he usually needs it, you'll look like a genius every time. If the bills are longer than the paychecks, give him some room to think and contemplate. If he or you lose your jobs, he's going to need room to think so he can figure out some possible next steps. If he gets some bad news about a close friend, relative, or his health, I know you will want to be there to support him. But find out first if he wants company or … yes, room to think.

The more we men can have room to think, the less pressure tends to build up in us. Even if we don't solve all the world's problems in the thinking room, we at least got a good start. We've explored some possibilities, and that's worth its weight in gold.

Room to Cave

Another room your man needs is a room in which to cave. It's a room for periodic hibernation, just as the name implies. A cave is a place where typically he can isolate himself from the stresses of life. It can even be an indoors space for men to play in; men absolutely need space to play. Some men have bigger caves than others, but size is not necessarily what matters most. What matters is that there's a cave that safe, warm, and stocked with chips, snacks, and his favorite drinks.

If you live in a small dwelling and there is not a room to designate as his cave, schedule cave times for him in the living room, den, or a bedroom. Even if it's not scheduled, work with him to make it a cave that he'll love. Sometimes he may even want to cave with you.

The cave is crucial for the man. It can be a place of recreation, creativity, or reading and reflection. It depends on the man. Some men like a big-screen TV and a pool table in their cave. The key is having a place at home in order to unplug from the outside world and all its stresses and demands.

My wife built me a cave. Well, not quite. She redesigned a room and created a wonderful cave for me with comfortable chairs, my computer monitor, books, speakers for music, and my photography equipment. The paint colors are soothing but masculine. The cow skin on the floor adds a touch that I love. My hats hang on a nice rack so I can grab one when I head out the door. And the lighting is low and warm, the way I like it. Her Warm Touches, LLC design business is a fringe benefit I get for being her man.

My man-cave is where I go every morning to think and pray and read and write. But it doubles as my play room. I get to work on my hobby in there while I'm listening to music, eating my favorite peanuts, and enjoying a cold St. Pauli Girl (non-alcoholic). Sheri has made it so comfortable for me that I have to pull myself out of there. The point is, try to create a room for caving that suits your man.

Room to Work

This may go without saying, but your man needs room to work. I know some men who work so much their wives can't give them any more room for it. But there are some wives who interrupt their men's work so much they put his performance in jeopardy.

Ladies, your man was made to work. In fact, long before God presented Adam to Eve, Adam worked. I'm not suggesting that work should come before marriage, but room to work makes for a happy marriage. If your man works from home, give him room to work. Don't make him have to choose between a home office and a coffee shop. If you have small kids and working from home is a challenge for him, you might have to divide up the house or create a schedule to take the kids to the library to give him room regularly.

If he works outside the home, then let him do his job. His work is a significant source of pride for him. That's good pride. "The one who is unwilling to work, shall not eat" (2 Thessalonians 3:10 NIV). A man who works to take care of his family feels a sense of pride when he can do it well and make a solid living. But if you're calling and texting him all day long, that's not helpful. He needs room to get it done, and your support of his craft and his livelihood make for a friendlier home environment.

Room to Be Real

Ladies, there's a final room the man you cover needs in his life. It's called room to be real. Most men have nowhere to express their fears, disappointments, and sadness. As a result, we often find ourselves wearing masks. The word the Bible uses for masks is the one from which we get the word *hypocrite*.

Jesus had real issues with hypocrites. He told the disciples in Matthew 6:1-18 not to be like the hypocritical Pharisees. They gave, prayed, and fasted with hypocrisy. In other words, they focused more on looking spiritual than on being spiritual. They managed their appearances to impress people, but they failed to nurture their souls toward authentic religion.

Men who don't have room to be real about their lives with the woman who is closest to them will develop a pattern of hypocrisy. I don't think it's usually mean-spirited. But it's just as dangerous. People who live in hypocrisy eventually begin to think they're normal and fine. That's what happens to many men. Pretending to be okay becomes a normal way of life, and it cuts off real relationship with a woman just as spiritual hypocrisy cuts off real relationship with God.

Ladies, you can give your man room to be real if you will not be shocked by anything he tells you. Can you handle his honesty about your weaknesses? Can he tell you when he feels you are not attending to him without you becoming defensive? If he says he's unfulfilled sexually and doing what honors God to be faithful to you, can you receive that without taking offense? Many men are not honest because the ladies in their lives won't give them room for honesty. So they stuff and pretend and sulk.

Ladies you hold the keys to the rooms. You have power to open doors no one can close and to close doors no one else can open (Revelation 3:7 NIV). If you use your keys to unlock the doors and open up rooms for your man to grow, expand, rest, recreate, work, and be real, what you'll find is a man with greater joy, balance, and gratitude for having you in his life.

Chapter 13 Reflections:

1. If the entire house is dedicated to the kids, the furniture, your projects, and who knows what else, your man is a forgotten entity. He needs space of his own. God designed men so that we compartmentalize our existence.

2. Your man needs a room in which to cave. It's a room for periodic hibernation, just as the name implies. A cave is a place where typically he can isolate himself from the stresses of life. It can even be an indoors space for men to play in; men absolutely need space to play.

3. Ladies, you can give your man room to be real if you will not be shocked by anything he tells you. Can you handle his honesty about your weaknesses? Can he tell you when he feels you are not attending to him without you becoming defensive?

A Few Final Thoughts

Ladies, thank you for reading all the way to the end of Cover Him! My sincere hope is that you've found this book to be a value-added resource. I hope each chapter felt like an eye- opening, coaching session that provided tools, fuel, and insights that you can use to improve your relationship with your him — the guy you are called to cover.

Now that you, hopefully, feel much more equipped with insights from the mind, heart, and experiences of a friend about men, I'd like to offer a few thoughts about your next moves with the man in your life!

Don't Coach Him

The field of coaching, including Life Coaching, Executive Coaching, Business Coaching, Relationship Coaching, etc. has grown to be a multi-billion dollar industry. It's made room for people with all sorts of passions, experiences, and expertise to develop professions along unconventional paths. I think it's awesome that genius can be shared across many areas of life in ways that allow more people to be supported, encouraged, and inspired to be their best.

But I offer this word of caution. Your man will resent feeling coached by you if you take a "coach approach" to your relationship with him. The best coaches offer accountability, help clients to focus and remain clear about their goals, and challenge them with perceptive questions that get at the heart of fears, hesitations, and procrastination (to name a few). Most people who have coaches hire them. They hire coaches because they're willing to pay someone who is unbiased to push them, offer the benefit of their years of expertise, and help them excel in specific areas of life, relationships, and career.

It's highly unlikely that the man you're called to cover is looking for you to be his coach. So be careful with the pep talks, the rah-rah, and the coaching styled inquiries: "So what are your options for moving forward? Have you thought about these three things?". That will likely land on him in a strange, perhaps condescending way. It'll make it difficult for him to feel relationally close to you. It's more likely that he will begin to distance himself from you emotionally.

Rather than use your new-found insights to become his new coach, make what you've learned a matter of prayer for him and for your relationship. Consider your new knowledge material for further exploration and understanding. Ask him for example, "Is it helpful to you if I pray for you without telling you? … *Cover Him* says, men need rooms in their lives. Is that true for you? Which of the rooms in the book would be helpful to you in our relationship? … What are your companionship needs? … How am I doing prioritizing you?" Make your insights a matter of discussion. Try to be as organic as possible. Let him know you're trying to learn how to cover him. There's no rush. Life's a journey.

Don't Throw Your Insights At Him

I'm not sure how to communicate this gently or clearly, so let me just jump right in. Have you ever had an experience where someone used all their newly acquired insights to remind you of all your failures or inadequacies? Or to give you an overly simplistic, fast track to getting your act together? I bet you remember exactly how it made you feel. Really, a little bit of knowledge can be a dangerous thing in the hands of the wrong person.

Statements like, "Now I know why you always do that."… "The book says, all men struggle with rejection if they're not getting enough sex. That's probably what's wrong with you." Ladies, be careful not to weaponize your insights. Don't try to fix the man you're called to cover. He may need some fixing; we all do. But trying to be his fixer will make the relationship all about you rather than about you together. Share your insights with him as a humble learner who is curious to learn, grow, and understand more. Ask him to teach you what you may not know about him, especially in the areas we discussed in the book. That's a much more effective approach than throwing your insights at him like spears looking for a target.

Be Patient With Him

This is always the hardest part about any growing relationship — patience. But as the apostle Paul said, "Love is patient." (1 Corinthians 13:1, NIV) Ladies, be patient with the man you are positioned to cover. I have no way of knowing how healthy or how unhealthy your relationship may be. So I certainly don't advocate patience in a relationship that's abusive on any level — verbally, physically, emotionally, or otherwise. Do not be patient with a man who is abusive just because you are now more equipped to understand his inner thoughts, feelings, and needs. His abusive ways are not your fault, nor are they your puzzle to solve. *Cover Him* is not perspective about abusive men. Throughout the book I've assumed healthy relationship with a healthy man about whom you need more understanding, given our differences as men and women.

If the man you are called to cover is honorable, God-fearing, and respectable, then be patient with the process. I encourage you to share *Cover Her* (my first book) with him. You may even want to compare notes from your separate readings of the two books. You'll know patience is the right direction if the following are true of him and your relationship:
1.) He honors and respects you. 2.) He's hungry to get better as a man, husband, father, and leader. 3.) He is genuinely seeking to grow in his relationship with God and welcomes the community found with like-spirited men. And of course, if you're already in a marriage relationship, weigh the requisite commitment to the sacred covenant. Be prayerful as you're being patient.

Be Clear With Him

Clarity is always better than confusion. Certainty is always better than uncertainty. It's better, my sister, for you to be clear with the man in your life. Be clear about your desire to know him better, to understand him better, to journey with him better. Be clear that you see covering him as part of a life-long journey of learning and an adventure that you are up for. Be clear that you will need his help — i.e. that you can't do it on your own without his patience, understanding, and communication.

Meet the Author

Rod Hairston, M.A., author of *Cover Him*, is the Senior Pastor of Messiah Community Church, just outside of Baltimore, MD. Along with a wonderful team of leaders, Pastor Rod is dedicated to seeing men and families experience wholeness and God's very best for their lives. He's driven by a desire to see people healed, strengthened, and equipped to show others the unconditional love of Christ.

For 14 seasons he invested his passion for men and families as chaplain and life coach of the NFL's Baltimore Ravens. There he earned two Super Bowl rings for his role in the Ravens' success as one of the NFL's premiere football organizations — an accomplishment and experience he cherishes.

When Rod is not teaching and preaching at Messiah or coaching the church's leaders, you'll find him speaking to men and married couples, around the country and on his iPad coaching NFL couples. He's also an avid photographer who never leaves home without his camera gear. When he's relaxing, it's behind a camera capturing landscapes and seascapes wherever his travels take him.

A graduate of Virginia Tech, Rod has been married for more than 28 years to Sheri, the love of his life and his closest friend. The couple has four adult children, whom they consider their *magnum opus* — their great work.

Cover Her is his first book. For more information, visit Rod's website, www.rodhairston.com and Messiah Community Church's website, www.messiahcc.org.

Notes

Chapter 3

[1] Myles Munroe, [Citation data needed for footnote]

Chapter 4

[2] "Who Are Sex Offenders?" csom.org, Accessed March 8, 2019, (http://www.csom.org/train/supervision/short/01_02_03.html)

[3] Sarah Hunter Murray, "How Sexual Rejection Really Impacts Relationships" www.PsychologyToday.com, Nov. 23, 2016, https://www.psychologytoday.com/us/blog/myths-desire/201611/how-sexual-rejection-really-impacts-relationships

Chapter 6

[4] Mark Goulston and John Ullmen, *Persuade Without Pushing and Gain Without Giving In* (New York, NY: Amacom, 2013), p. 00-00.

[5] Citation needed for Nielson statistic.

[6] Citation needed for statistic.

Chapter 10

[7] Henry Cloud & John Townsend, *Boundaries* (Grand Rapids, MI: Zondervan, 2017), p. 00

Chapter 13

[8] Mike Yarbrough, www.wolfandiron.com

CPSIA information can be obtained
at www.ICGtesting.com
Printed in the USA
LVHW052351300820
664592LV00017B/2236